RECLAIM YOUR STORY

Renew Your
Health and
Wellness through
the Power of
Storytelling

DR. CARRIE JAROSINSKI

Reclaim Your Story: Renew Your Health and Wellness through the Power of Storytelling
Carrie Jarosinski

© 2022, Carrie Jarosinski
Chapter and Cover Illustrations © 2022, August Learning Solutions

Published by August Learning Solutions
Cleveland, OH

www.augustlearningsolutions.com

All rights reserved. This book or any portion thereof may not be reproduced or used in any manner whatsoever, including but not limited to photocopying, scanning, digitizing, or any other electronic storage or transmission, without the express written permission of the publisher.

Print ISBN: 978-1-941626-53-5
EPUB ISBN: 978-1-941626-56-6

Printed in the United States of America

26 25 24 23 22   1 2 3 4 5 6 7 8 9 10

CONTENTS

A Note to the Reader		v
CHAPTER ONE	The Power of Storytelling	1
CHAPTER TWO	The Storyteller	7
CHAPTER THREE	Setting the Scene	17
CHAPTER FOUR	Supporting Actors in Your Story	51
CHAPTER FIVE	Act One	83
CHAPTER SIX	The Dramatic Arc	109
CHAPTER SEVEN	Act Two	185
CHAPTER EIGHT	Writing Your Future Script	219
CHAPTER NINE	Curtain Call	247
ENCORE	Additional Reading to Further Support Your Intellectual Health and Well-Being	261
APPENDIX	Values List	277

A NOTE TO THE READER

I am so happy that you are excited to take a step in your wellness journey with me. Thank you for allowing me the opportunity to work with you. I wanted to share a little bit about myself and this book before we begin our work.

I always wanted to be a teacher; however, my academic preparation did not take me there right away. I actually began my career as a massage therapist. This stoked my fascination to learn more about the human body and pushed me in the direction of the nursing profession. I completed my associate degree in nursing and worked in long-term care, helping older adults in the end stages of their life. I just had this feeling that I was not done with my education, that there was so much more information out there that I could soak up and learn so that I could better help those that I served. I continued my education in the field of nursing, completing my bachelor's degree and with that taking on a new role in public health. Public health is a great sector of our health care industry because its focus is on primary prevention—stopping disease before it starts by teaching folks how to live their healthiest life. In other words, education! Appreciating the opportunity that lies with teaching others about health, I continued on to complete my master's degree in nursing with an emphasis in education, which led me to my role as a faculty member at the very technical college that I attended to complete my first nursing degree. Yes, I came full circle. With a recognized love of both education and nursing, I completed my doctoral degree with an emphasis in population health; it is this beautiful amalgamation of both worlds to help and to teach. Throughout my academic and practice journey I have become a Certified Nurse Educator (CNE), a Certified Wellness Practitioner (CWP), a group fitness instructor, and health coach. I love to use my educational preparation and technical expertise to help others be the best iteration of themselves. As a nurse, I appreciate the medical conditions that can harm our health. As an educator, I love sharing new information with others to help folks learn and grow. As a wellness practitioner and health coach, I embrace a holistic and client empowering stance to maximize potential wherever that may exist for the individual in that space and time. I am so grateful for the opportunity to help those that are seeking wellness.

I wrote this book to continue to help others appreciate the vastness of health and wellness and understand what that really "looks like" in action so that they may become the best iteration of themselves. While all the information in this book is rooted in best practice evidence, I wanted to ensure the information was digestible and meaningful to folks. In doing so, I have taken a lighthearted, conversational tone with the reader as opposed to that of an academic tone. I feel like we all learn better when we are comfortable and in a safe space. I wrote this book envisioning my friends and I sitting around my dining room table, just having a conversation. I hope you enjoy the content and can easily apply it to your daily life, my friends.

One more thing: this book was meant to be written in, so feel free to jot down notes in the margin, write your ideas into the free spaces, or grab your own notebook to lay out your ideas if you are reading the e-version of this book so that you can go back, reflect, and put the pieces of your manuscript together by the end of this book. You will also see a few QR codes placed throughout the text for ease of access to outside materials. To utilize the QR codes, scan the code with your phone's camera to be taken to the additional content. Thank you for sharing your journey with me.

ACKNOWLEDGMENTS

Writing this book was definitely not arduous, nor a labor of love, it was genuinely fun! The seedling idea for this book was planted by my son. During one of our conversations he reflected that while health was taught to him in school, wellness was not. This got me thinking. If we are not teaching wellness then how healthy can we actually be? Thank you Dylan for giving me the gift of inspiration. During the writing of this book I was gently guided by my daughter. You see, sometimes my wellness slips out of balance. Thank you Jillian for calling that out and keeping me in check. Thank you to all of my unicorns that never cease to amaze me with their continuous love, support, check-ins, and cheerleading. It fosters my resilience and perseverance in all that I do. And finally, thank you to the talented team at August Learning Solutions for believing in this project and in me so that we could bring this seedling to fruition. Be well.

CHAPTER ONE

THE POWER OF STORYTELLING

Stories evoke deep inspiration, sadness, hope for humanity, and fear of humanity. Storytelling is a powerful tool that has been used through the ages. It is used to teach the next generation what to avoid and how to be successful, it warns us of our sins of the past, it is leveraged to prevent repeat failures, and is shared to rouse joy, wonder, love, awe, and hope. Our ancestors drew pictures on walls to tell a story; elders told bedtime yarns to babes; pen was put to paper in fables with embedded morals that were written to entertain and teach us. Storytelling is interwoven in our human nature. Humans seem to have this intrinsic pull to share our stories, others' stories, and past stories though words, pictures, art, gossip, movies, song, theatre, love letters, gaslighting, poetry. We are separated by the animal kingdom in this power; this is how we impart cumulative knowledge generation after generation. It is how our pool of knowledge grows deeper with each passing generation, if only we harness that power.

I wrote this book to share just a part of my story with you in my journey to wellness. It is my humbled hope that I might positively impact and support you in your own journey. But this is just one story. It is important to wrap yourself in the power of positive storytelling through friends, family, workplaces, your environment, and so much more, because we are the sum of these stories. They influence us every moment of our life and in every decision we make. Yes, we ultimately make our own choices and determine our own path in this world, but the stories that surround us are profoundly influential, and startlingly, most of us are unaware of these stories or their impacts on our journey.

Now, maybe you are thinking, "Yeah, I can see your point, but I'm not so sure that storytelling is actually as powerful as you think it is, Carrie." OK, let's start from the beginning. Think about a favorite movie or song—something that inspires you or moves you to emotion. Have that in mind yet? Now think about the story it tells you, and then think why it's your favorite. Personally, I love the movie *Moana*, because the story behind it is of this young girl that realizes from an early age that she is more capable and has a larger future than anyone else ever imagined. Of course, she experiences self-doubt, losses, and discouragement along the way, but in the end she follows her heart and passions to fulfill her true potential. It's not one of my favorites because it is a Disney movie that cost $150 million to make, or because the songs are awesome (OK, that's part of it—they really are—they're on my playlist), but because the story resonates and inspires me to be a better version of me, to keep searching for my maximal potential even when I feel beat down. If storytelling wasn't so pivotal or impactful to the human race, Disney would not make a profit of $4.5 billion per year.

Let me share just a couple of other stories to get you thinking about this power. Ever hear of Humans of New York (HONY)? I sure hope so, and if not, go to social media and start following this. You will be brought to tears on a regular basis through the power of storytelling. I will give you a high-level overview of this and then do a deeper dive into one of his stories. This guy named Brandon Stanton decided to do a photography project back in 2010; his goal was to photograph 10,000 random New Yorkers on the street. Along the way he started to interview those that he was photographing, which turned into a blog. He now has more than 20 million followers on social media. And he literally just takes a photo and shares a story of ordinary people he happens upon. These stories are heart-wrenching and inspirational, tragic and mesmerizing. And remember, these are just ordinary folks he stumbles upon in NYC. Why does Brandon do this? Why does he have millions of followers reading his blog? Because everyone has a story that is powerful that we can learn from and that influences us, if we just stop to listen and learn. If you think storytelling isn't powerful, chat with Brandon and his 20 million followers.

Sometimes the folks that Brandon happens upon are not so ordinary. One in particular, Stephanie Johnson, quickly captured the hearts of HONY followers. Stephanie, otherwise known as Tanqueray in her stripper days, shared her story with Brandon and the world. After photographing and interviewing her for the initial HONY blog, the world wanted to hear more of Stephanie's story, and Brandon responded. He sat down with Stephanie and over the course of 20 interviews shared a 32-part story on his blog. Her brutally raw story is filled with mobsters, goings-on of affluent nightclubs, scandalous high-ranking officials, drug addiction, hard race conversations, and brutally frank speech about being a stripper making "white girl money as a Black girl" in the 1970s. During the 20-interview blog installment Stephanie's health was quite poor, so Brandon decided to start a GoFundMe to help Stephanie pay for her medical bills. Listening to her compelling storytelling, waiting on bated breath for each new installment, folks all over the world donated and raised over $3 million to help her. Strangers sending money from across the globe to help an aging Black woman, and in turn supporting belief in humanity. This is powerful stuff.

And storytelling is not just words. Stories are conveyed through so many different mediums. I remember touring a Holocaust museum in Germany. The grounds were somber; grief hung in the air. There was an unnatural stillness and quiet that was unsettling to the soul. The heart weighed heavier with each building we entered on the grounds, each hollow room telling a story of loss, sadness, indignity, and a loathsome lack of humanity through its echoes. One building was the "health intake" room where Jews, homosexuals, political dissidents, and other marginalized groups that did not align with Nazi ideology were taken once entering the compound. In this room there stood an exam table and a height measurement tool on the wall. Just behind the measuring tool, there was a small wooden cutout with a sliding door on it. As prisoners would stand shoulders against the wall for the examination, the door would slide open, and a Nazi soldier would shoot the prisoner in the back of the head. It was done this way for fear of how the soldiers' distraught feelings over the continuous slaughter might affect their well-being, offering them a bit of detachment from their horrendous acts. Despair for humanity saturated the air when looking upon this spartan room. In yet another building there was a room completely full of big and tiny shoes. Shoes that were collected from the men, women, and children that entered the camp but did not leave. This story of inhumanity is powerful too.

Stories can evoke deep inspiration, sadness, hope for humanity, and fear of humanity. Stories are why we sit around a campfire with friends, share a glass of wine at book club, pay $20 for a tub of popcorn and sit down at the theatre for the newest movie, follow travel bloggers on Instagram, and snuggle up with a big book of fairy tales to read to our kiddos at night. Storytelling is at the very root of our being. It can make us better or beat us down. It has the power to heal and the power to destroy. We all have a story to share with others, and more importantly, we have a story we share with ourselves inside our own heads. And that is where this wellness journey begins. I hope to use this power of storytelling to help you begin our adventure together. Throughout this book, I offer a high-level overview of some of the many components that support a wellness journey. Know that these topics are rooted in evidence, meaning they are founded in an abundance of up-to-date research and current best practice guidelines. As an educator and health coach, I use these concepts daily to support others' journeys to wellness and in this book, I am sharing them with you. At the end of the book, I will offer further reading resources for those of you interested in deepening your knowledge in any of these topic areas.

The show must go on!

Next up, we will take a look at how the stories we tell ourselves can shape not only what we think about ourselves, but how we act!

CHAPTER TWO

THE STORYTELLER

8 Reclaim Your Story

Maybe you're starting to wonder "what's my story"? Excellent! Well then, for the first step in your personal storytelling journey, you need to travel inside your own head. This is not as scary or as difficult as you might think, but I am going to ask that you be brave in this journey by journaling some thoughts and feelings as we go through the concepts. It can be difficult to take the time to stop and reflect on what it is that is actually going on inside of your own mind. So often, we are on autopilot throughout the day. We wake up and before our feet hit the floor, we have an endless stream of "to-dos." We contemplate what to wear, what we are going to make for breakfast, how we need to juggle our time between meetings, kids, the gym, school, doctor appointments, grocery store runs, and making everyone happy and comfortable in between all of those "to dos." It is exhausting, and that is on the easy, mundane days! During stressful times, it is even more of a challenge. However, it is in that autopilot zone that we really do not acknowledge what we are telling ourselves at any given moment, and that can be either helpful or hurtful to our well-being.

Here is where this stuff gets good. Let me share a little secret about the role of the "storyteller" or "narrator" of life. It's you. Surprise! We are going to take a hard look at identifying what you have been and are currently telling yourself up to this point (most often unbeknownst to you). This is the keystone of any wellness journey; it is vitally important to acknowledge and appreciate before you attempt any sort of wellness behavior change.

Your narrator is this little voice in your head that pretty much goes nonstop. This voice is even more powerful than the stories in the first chapter, because it is the story of you—past you, current you, and future you. It can be your best friend or your worst enemy. But here is the beautiful part of it all: you are in charge of it, and you get to control this running dialogue. It only takes an awakening to this narration to take control. First, let's talk a little bit about this inner dialogue, often called self-talk. As I mentioned, it is playing in the background pretty much all the time. Most often, this running dialogue is about mundane things like what is on your to-do list, how and when you are going to execute this to-do list, a narration of what is happening in the given moment, a reimagining of past moments, dreaming of future events . . . all of those kinds of things. However, there is this insidious element that can be dangerous. It's often called the inner critic, but I affectionately like to call it your inner jerk. It's this inner voice that whispers judgment in your ear ever so slightly, so that you may not even register it. For example, when you get out of the shower and look in the mirror, it is that little voice in the back of your mind that says "ugh" as you turn away. It is that little narrator that says, "Well that was stupid, what was I thinking?" when you get home from work and realize you didn't thaw out the chicken for dinner tonight. It is the storyteller that says, "There's no way I can break up with Cheetos, they're the only thing I can count on when the going gets tough, and life really sucks right now." It's the little jerk that tells you, "I'm such a bad mom, I can't believe I forgot to send along little Liam's lunch money," or "I am sure I blew that test, if I weren't so lazy I would have just studied more and then I would have passed." It's your own personal little judge, jury, and executioner, hanging out with you at any given moment, creeping its way into your self-talk. This seductive little sleepy voice plays off of your inner fears, worries, and anxieties without you even noticing. It is a slippery little antagonist that we sacrifice far too much power to, and here's the thing: when you keep allowing this negative narrator to be a jerk to you, you will start to believe what it is saying. Over time, it can cause shame, anxiety, sadness, and even depression, and it is an internal threat to any type of wellness behavior change you may want to enact now or in the future.

Maybe you are thinking that the shame that is produced by this inner critic can affect behavior change for the better. "It works for me!", some folks say. If I tell myself I'm stupid for not studying and that I deserved the F on that test, then maybe I will do better on the next one! Here's the thing about shame. You may see a quick bump in behavior change after the shaming commences, but it is unsustainable. Let me share some examples. The person that is forced to wear a sandwich board on the corner of a busy intersection shaming them for stealing donut holes at the 7-Eleven is not going to have any sort of sustainable behavior change; stealing will continue until the original motivator for the theft is addressed. Shaming your child for getting bad grades may result in a better test score on the next exam, but the following report card will be the same, if not worse. Shaming yourself for "messing up another relationship" may get you to change your behavior on your next first and second dates, but it will not make you a better sustained partner in the future. One thing I can promise you is that putting in the hard work of these wellness practices that we will discuss in this book, and putting aside the shame, anxiety, and sadness that the inner critic induces, will help you to be the best iteration of you.

Here is some great news: there is an antidote to this problem. I would like to formally introduce you to your inner antagonist. "Carrie, meet your inner jerk. Inner jerk, this is Carrie." This introduction, this moment of awakening to your negative critic, is the first step in harnessing the power of your own storytelling so that you take control over the quality of your life. This is your "pay no attention to the man behind the curtain!" moment—once you expose the inner critic, you take away its negative power over you, your actions, and ultimately your health.

So this is the very first step in your own storytelling process—asking the question, "Who am I and what's the story I've been telling myself all these years?" And here is the answer: you are who you tell yourself you are. Marcus Aurelius said that "the happiness of your life depends upon the quality of your thoughts: therefore, guard accordingly," and he could not be truer in this sentiment. If you tell yourself you are stupid, a bad partner, fat, lazy, too tired to play with your kids, too old, untrustworthy, or any other negative story line, that is what will come to fruition in your demeanor, actions, and ultimately your health status. However, if you can catch this antagonist in action and flip the switch to make it a protagonist, you will conversely see well-being come to fruition first in your attitude, then in your actions, and finally in your overall well-being.

Let me use an example to highlight these impacts. You messed up a big project at work and now your boss is displeased with you. What is your inner narrator telling you? Is it saying you are a screw-up and you should just quit? Or is it saying that, yeah, you might have messed up, but this is a learning moment, and now you know how to do the project properly so the next time it is your responsibility, you can do a better job? This is flipping the story line by hijacking your inner critic storyteller before it can make you feel even worse about the problem and yourself, sending you into a self-fulfilling prophecy of failure.

Now some of you could be thinking, "Oh boy, this is some Stuart Smalley kind of stuff." For those of you that are not familiar with Stuart, let me explain. Stuart Smalley was a character on *Saturday Night Live* in the 90s whose catchphrase was, "I'm good enough, I'm smart enough, and doggone it, people like me!" He would say this while gazing into a full-length mirror as one of his daily affirmations. It was hysterical. For those of you that have never seen Stuart, YouTube it; you will not be sad. I digress. This is not a Stuart Smalley intervention I am talking about here. Stuart's goal was to build self-esteem through his outwardly artificial praises while covering up his bombastic internal sufferings. Catching the inner critic storyteller is not about building your self-esteem to cover up self-identified weaknesses (more on that later)—rather, it is about stopping internal self-harm so we can begin to heal from a positive space, which will serve as a foundation to create sustainable behavior changes.

I want to share a story with you about my own journey—about this inner voice in action and how debilitating it can be. I started my wellness journey because I began suffering from panic attacks in my 30s. Pretty common these days, actually. Over 40 million people in the United States have a problem with anxiety disorders. That is a lot of people, but when it's happening to you, it feels like you are completely alone, you are debilitated, and it is terrifying, both mentally and physically. Those that suffer from panic attacks often start to curb their actions to avoid further attacks, which quickly spirals out of control by way of self-limiting actions. This eventually morphs into a fear of fear.

My panic attacks centered around driving. At first the trigger was just driving on the interstate, but as I allowed the fear to take me over, my world quickly shrunk to the point where I would avoid driving over bridges and wouldn't even take quick jaunts to the next town over so as to avoid any potential of an attack. I was so paralyzed with fear that I became dependent on others to drive me places that I wanted to go, or I simply avoided doing things that I needed to drive for. What I didn't realize was that my inner critic was whispering things to continuously strengthen and solidify this fear into my very being. "I hate driving," "I'm not a good driver," "I can't drive," "I would never be able to drive myself to see my friend for a girls' weekend"—these were just a few of my thoughts, a tiny sliver of my antagonist's running mantra behind the scenes. I actually became this fear. It became who I was and how I identified myself. This storyteller was quietly narrating a self-fulfilling prophecy that forced my world to become smaller and smaller, shrinking my abilities and my self-worth. I realized that this was not the person I wanted to be, but I had no idea where to start, how to conquer my fears, or how to get "healthy" enough to stop my fear-of-fear cycle.

Reflecting back, I now look at my panic attacks as a gift. Without my body and mind screaming for that come-to-Jesus moment, I would have stayed on autopilot and my world would have continued to shrink into my negative space. My journey to wellness is fraught with many plot twists and painful character developments, which I will share with you throughout this book as a way to better explain some of these concepts. It is my hope that you can start to reflect on your own plot twists and character developments, too. I liken this journey to a domino pattern. One domino spurs action to the next and then the next for all of us. I am not quite certain what that full pattern of fallen dominos is yet, but I know it will be beautiful when I can get to that aerial view. I hope your wellness journey will be, too; it's how you really get to know yourself and then propel yourself into cascading and cumulative positive behavior change.

As we begin this journey together, remember to be brave. As you work on one area, you will probably identify other areas you can improve upon. This is a journey, a process, and one that will not ever stop (at least hopefully!). Keep in mind that wellness is a continuous quality improvement process that is a private endeavor in getting to know yourself on a deeper level and being able to identify and articulate your needs, aspirations, and inspirations. Identifying your inner narrator is the first step in this journey; it is the keystone. Without turning off that autopilot and actually awakening to yourself and your thoughts, you will not be able to effect any kind of meaningful behavior change, or if you do, it will not be sustainable. So please do not skip this part; it is the first step on the first brick of that yellow brick road.

Now it's your turn. Take the next few hours to really notice what you are thinking. It is a pretty quiet voice at first, but once you start paying attention to it, you might be surprised. A good way to begin to listen to your self-talk is to sit quietly and just try to not think. When you try to not think, you will be deluged with thoughts—I promise! Once you are tuned into that storyteller, dig through the autopilot narration of the mundane daily activities to identify if there are any of those quiet whispers of judgment and worry. In the following pages, I would like you to write down what your narrator is telling you over these next few hours. It doesn't have to be paragraphs, but jot down the sentiment of your thoughts. Take note of how often you catch that inner voice talking. What is the common theme? Is it mostly negative or positive? Is it a chatty little beast racing through your mind, or a quiet and calm whisper floating atop a still pond? Is it ruminating on past events or worrying about the future? Jot those notes down as your formal introduction to your narrator and your awakening moment.

Self-talk notes:

Finally, I would like you to reflect on who you are and what your story is. Imagine you are introducing yourself to your inner narrator and introducing your inner narrator to yourself by answering these three questions.

- How do you describe yourself?
- What's your story?
- Who are you?

How easily did those answers flow? Was it more difficult to answer these questions after you acknowledged your inner narrator? Were the answers different from what you thought they would be? Did your story or your thoughts of yourself change at all? Were there conflicting ideas and information? After you have that written down, we can start to take a closer look at how to set the scene for the next step in your journey.

**For those of you reading the e-book version, I sure wish this could be a fillable field for you, but until I get my wish, please write these down in a journal or notebook so that you can continue to reflect back on your thoughts and ideas throughout reading this book and long afterward; that way, you can measure your growth over time. There will be lots of opportunities where I will ask you to do some self-reflection throughout the book, jot down notes, and then reflect back on them, so it will be nice for you to be able to refer back to those in your handy notebook during each of those exercises and to see how they all come together at the end of your journal.

The show must go on!

Now that you have a better understanding of your story, or the story you have been telling yourself, we will move on to think about letting go of some false constructs we have built for ourselves and therefore devote some of that wasted energy into creating a safe space to learn and grow from.

CHAPTER THREE

SETTING THE SCENE

I hope your formal introduction to your inner narrator was insightful. Take a look at what you wrote down in your reflection at the end of the last chapter. Did you spend a lot of time worrying about the future, ruminating over past events, or were you living in the now? Most of us spend the bulk of our time in the future or in the past. Not a bad thing per se, but good to make a note of as we continue our journey together. Were you more of a "Negative Nellie" or do you have more of a "Positive Pollyanna" perspective on life?

> ☐ I trended toward Nellie
>
> ☐ I trended toward Pollyanna

If your self-talk leaned more toward the positive and supportive, that is great news; you have a solid foundation from which to launch your wellness storytelling journey. If it was leaning more toward the Nellie end of the spectrum, not a problem! Acknowledging the little beastie takes its power away and offers you the space to grow and change for the positive, and it too serves as a great space to launch your journey from. We all have characteristics of both positive and negative thinking; we just have to figure out how to balance the configuration so that it lands more squarely in the "Pollyanna" camp as opposed to dear old "Nellie."

Keep in mind that last chapter's self-talk exercise was just a tiny snapshot of your life. Reflect on if there were other things happening at the time you listened to your self-talk that could have shifted the balance between positive and negative. Was this a "normal" day for you or were there things happening that were either exciting or stressful that could influence the overall trends of the narration? Personally, when it is cold and dark with not-so-great weather or when I am overtired, I tend to be far more negative in my self-talk than when it is sunny and I can be outdoors without eight layers on (not great to be a lifelong resident of Wisconsin, I know). As you continue this practice, try to note those triggers that move you in one direction or the other. Maybe it is the weather, lack of or too much sleep, demanding workdays, stressful relationships, or lengthy to-do lists. No matter what it is, tracking the trends can help you more quickly identify the inner critic and turn the ship around to pick up poor Pollyanna waiting for you on the other side of the riverbank and drop Nellie in your wake.

This exercise may have been a first awakening to self-talk listening for you, or a gentle reminder if you have already been practicing the skill of listening to self-talk. As you move forward in your wellness journey, these awakening moments should occur more frequently so that you become more in tune with your storytelling process. This isn't a "one-and-done" type of exercise. It takes time to cultivate, so allow yourself the space to develop and hone this skill. You can make a conscious effort to practice it during mundane tasks like while you are doing dishes, walking the dog, driving to the soccer pitch, brushing your teeth, or watching TV to easily fit the practice into your life. The more often you practice, the more it will become a habit, and the more you can catch that little antagonist from whispering negativity to you.

Now that you know who the lead actor and narrator of your story is, we are going to explore setting your scene. If you can't tell by now, I love stories. I love reading, watching movies, chatting with girlfriends, telling bedtime stories, you name it. In high school I participated in all of the musicals; I was in awe of the props being built, the choreography coming together, beautiful costumes galore, and the pit orchestra stitching together scene after scene. Sure, musicals can be entertaining with just the actors on the stage and a pianist, but what makes the story so rich are all of these moving parts merging together alongside the actors to deliver a beautiful work of art. To this day, one of my favorite activities is going to the theatre. When done well, it moves something inside of me. I am going to assume it has that effect on a lot of people since more than 14 million people go to a Broadway show each year. With this power in mind, let's work on setting your stage so that your daily life activities merge together synchronously and move you to awe and wonderment, and you can create a masterful story of your life filled with beauty.

In the story setting of your wellness journey, the first concept we need to chat about is the false dichotomy of the good versus bad storyline we narrate to ourselves. No one is all good and no one is all bad; this is not a Nicolas Cage movie. We all have our flaws. This is tied to the narrator issue we spoke about in the previous chapter: When you catch yourself saying things like, "I am the worst at cooking, I don't know why I even try anymore," you are putting yourself in a negative box where there is no hope to grow or change. Sure, you might not be able to make a Pop-Tart without burning it right now, but that does not mean you don't have the capacity to grow, change, and ultimately not be horrible. Who knows, crème brûlée may be in your future someday! Or at least the mastering of a beautifully browned cinnamon Pop-Tart without setting off the smoke alarm. Either can be a success. It's kind of like kung fu. You can be a Bruce Lee, a Chuck Norris, or a Po the Panda. I think each is equally awesome in their own way, despite their different skill levels. Each of them stuck with it, did it their own way, and blazed their own trail to satisfaction and internal happiness.

Part of my inner critic constantly reminds me that I am "the least bendy person ever." OK, it's not just my inner narrator telling me this—I have literally said this out loud to anyone who will listen. I think the only time I may have been able to touch my toes was when I was an infant, but alas, I have no photographic proof of this. It was the 70s and I was the third child. In grade school gym class during the fitness testing, I was the one who didn't come anywhere close to touching my toes (neither could my kids, by the way, so I am saying this is a genetic problem), garnering a disapproving stare from Ms. Beggs. As I grew into adulthood I continued with this mantra to my detriment. Mind you, I participated in all kinds of sports and exercises with the exception of, you guessed it, anything that had anything to do with flexibility. I had completely psyched myself out so badly that I simply threw up my arms in disgust and gave up the notion that I could ever even attempt to stretch. Not even for two minutes, because I was so bad at it. As you can imagine I grew older, and this didn't work out so well for me. I started getting injuries, my flexibility worsened (if you can believe it), and I found myself begrudgingly at the physical therapist's office begging for help with chronic hip pain. But with age (and injury), I was able to catch that inner critic and change the scene to create a new story line by telling myself that I was not the worst and I actually had the potential to be better. So where am I at now? If you guessed that I am trekking down to the local yoga studio doing the King Pigeon pose, you are sorely mistaken, though I thank you for your supportive thoughts and belief in me.

Here is the thing—you don't have to have these artificial, dichotomous "I'm great" or "I suck" notions. It is totally OK to be mediocre at something. Just flipping my mindset from "I am the least bendy person EVER" to "I may be bendy challenged, but I am going to try for the sake of my health to be a bit more flexible" is powerful. Do you see the magic there? This is the power of self-efficacy. Meaning I have the belief that I can actually make a change and find some success with that change. Just one teeny tiny flip of a little switch of "setting the stage for behavior change" in taking control of that inner narrator can lead to a better version of me. Not a better yoga student than Joe Schmoe next door; just a better version of me. So, since I know you are all wondering where I am at in my hand-to-toe quest . . . I am about at shin height. I shut down my inner antagonist so that I no longer tell myself I am the worst ever, and when I start to say that out loud to Joe Schmoe, I catch myself and change what comes out of my mouth to something gentler, like, "I am bendy challenged, but I am working on it!" I reframe this topic in a more positive light, giving myself the space to just be OK with something as long as I am making an effort at getting better (setting the scene). I'm OK with my toe quest for right now, even though it may be lackluster to most, but I continue to work on it because I know that it will help prevent more injuries and hopefully even make me feel better in the process. So, most days of the week, I set aside anywhere from 5 to 15 minutes to just stretch (sustained behavior change). And even if I don't get any more bendy in adopting this wellness practice, it is 5 to 15 minutes of quiet time to myself to support my health and to support me being the best version of me that I can be, and that is what matters. You know, I am probably

Setting the Scene 23

as bendy as Po the Panda, but he sure was able to become the Dragon Warrior and do the Wuxi Finger Hold move to defeat Tai Lung in the end now, wasn't he?

What is one of your false dichotomies that you tell yourself? This is something you say either out loud or to yourself: things like, "I'm just not good at XYZ," or "I give up on trying because I will never achieve XYZ." Write that here:

_____
_____
_____

Now think about how you can reframe this statement to be a little less black and white or a little less mean to yourself. Write that out here:

_____
_____
_____

In addition to reframing your inner critic, there are certain concrete activities that you can do to set the scene for yourself, no matter what your wellness goal is. These activities will help build internal qualities that support any wellness behavior change goals that you are motivated to venture toward. Most importantly, setting the scene with these activities can support *sustainable* behavior change which, since this is why I am assuming you are reading this book, this is what you are after!

But first, before we dive into those scene setting activities, I wanted to take a moment to talk about the elephant in the "wellness goal" room. You may be thinking, "Boy, I bought this book because I wanted to get in shape to run a 5K or lose 10 pounds and all Carrie is talking about is this 'head stuff.' Come on already, I want to get healthy!" Here we go. Whenever someone says "I want to get healthy," most often the intent driving that statement is, "I want to move more" or "I want to eat better," with a goal of losing weight or changing their physical body in a certain way. I get it. Many folks have some pounds they want to take off, or some curves they want curvier, or some curves they want less curvy. Many of us have body image issues; guess what—me too! I am the lightest weight I have been since high school because of some hard work that I have already put in. But here's the thing. There are still things I am not ecstatic about and there will always be things like that. I have stretch marks that will never go away—thanks to eating my way through my pregnancies, my weight distribution is not where I want it to be—I can't change genetics, and I really do not have much in terms of muscle strength—OK, I can do something about that one. But the moral of the story is recalling that wellness is a continuous quality improvement project with no end. That is why it is a journey and not a destination, my friends! No one is perfect, we all have differences that we consider to be "flaws," but we can rejoice in these differences as they serve to pave our road for the journey ahead. The strength for our journey is found by choosing to see these differences as opportunities for growth and uniquenesses to our being. Rejoicing in these opportunities starts with our storytelling. So, it does not matter if your wellness journey goals are to lose 10 or 200 pounds, walk to the mailbox or run a marathon, be a kinder person or just a little bit less crabby with others, to become enlightened or to begin healing from past traumas. It all starts with flipping your story to one that begins with positivity and strength, aka "head stuff." Without that, you cannot sustain behavior change to meet any goals you may set for yourself. I also hope that you come to see by the end of this book that the term "health" is not just about physical health. Sure, it plays a big role, but there are so many more considerations that go into setting the stage of this storyline, all of which are needed to realize any physical health goals. More on that later.

Onward to paving the road for your journey. These activities we are stage setting for are all interrelated. You can pick and choose one or two of these to start to work on, but keep in mind that the more of these activities you can practice and embrace, the more impactful, beautiful, and gripping your story line plot will be. You will probably find that when you start working on one of these activities, others may present themselves as the next logical steps in your script. Let them unfold naturally like the beautiful scenes that they are. If you try to do too much too quickly, your audience (you at this point) will get overwhelmed and tune out. If you try to take a prescriptive path that someone else tells you to take, it will be disingenuous and end poorly. Identify which of these activities you want to or are able to work on, strengthen that one area, then when you are ready, move on to the next one that feels right for you. There is no "31 days to wellness" or "act in the next 5 minutes to earn the next badge" in this book. It is you, your journey, your story, and you are the one telling it; you are in charge. I am just offering you some suggestions to help you along your way. I just want to be your Sherpa.

The first activity we will discuss for setting your stage is forgiveness of both self and others. Didn't see that one coming, did you? Forgiveness is literally defined as a "conscious, deliberate decision to release feelings of resentment or vengeance toward a person or group who has harmed you, regardless of whether they actually deserve your forgiveness" (University of California Berkeley Greater Good Science Center, 2021). I would like you to reflect on this: "regardless of whether they actually deserve your forgiveness." This is the key to forgiveness. The other guy is going to do what the other guy is going to do. You have no impact on others' choices. You are only in control of your choices. It's about you, your journey, your healing, not "them."

Think about ways you have harmed yourself and those who have harmed you. To embark on this topic, I want you to reflect on a couple of things. First, can you make a conscious decision to let go of those angry feelings that you might have about yourself? Look back on your life and determine if there is anything you did that might make you feel resentful. Maybe your hurt was directed toward someone else. Maybe you hurt yourself in a physical or emotional way. Maybe you didn't realize you were hurting yourself but recently had an awakening to that pain from an inner narrator. Second, can you make a conscious decision to let go of those angry feelings and resentment toward those that have harmed you in your life, either intentionally or not?

Forgiveness is quite the powerful tool because it releases you from the past. So often, we recycle and reread old scripts. Did you notice in your awakening to the inner narrator that some of your thoughts were rumination about past events playing and replaying? While we can learn from the old scripts, to prevent making the same mistakes over again, sometimes we can get lost in a vicious cycle telling ourselves these old storylines that no longer serve us. Looking in that rear view mirror at all of the woulda, coulda, shoulda's prevents us from forgiving, living in the present, and moving forward. Rehashing these old story lines impacts our lives, and it simply isn't useful, helpful, or wholesome to keep going back to this ruminating space. They are just thoughts perseverating through our minds. Forgiveness can allow you to truly see these old scripts as just that: thoughts, old thoughts that are neither concrete nor tangible. By identifying these past thoughts as nothing concrete, it helps us to relinquish their power over us, our emotions, our actions, and our state of well-being.

The act of forgiveness can free your mind and your heart from anger that only serves to hurt you. Forgiveness is for the forgiver, not the person being forgiven. Think of it this way. Your heart is like this big, beautiful, old rose bush in your backyard. If you prune back all of the drought-stricken dead branches and leaves, you offer up space for sunlight to shine in upon it, resulting in new growth and bigger, better blossoms in the future. Forgiveness is that act of pruning so that you can grow bigger, stronger, and more beautiful throughout your life.

Here is the science behind forgiveness. It makes you happier. Brooding over past hurts from self or others just keeps you in the past and in a state of pain. Releasing guilt, anger, and frustration makes room for feelings of peace, happiness, and contentment. Those that forgive have lesser rates of anxiety and depression, have healthier, stronger, and longer lasting relationships, and have less stress, resulting in strengthened physical, emotional, and mental well-being. Forgiveness heals. Nelson Mandela was jailed and tortured for almost three decades for the simple act of championing humanity. Upon his release, he offered his forgiveness to those that committed these acts against him. Let me ask you this rhetorical question: if Nelson Mandela can forgive his captors for torture, imprisonment, and the loss of three decades worth of opportunity, might you be able to find it in your heart to forgive those that have pained you? Or to forgive yourself for past offenses? Something to chew on the next time you are ruminating. Refusing forgiveness keeps you in your own prison, a prison of the past. Only you can free yourself; absolutely no one else can do this for you.

Looking back on my younger years, there has been much to forgive, both in myself and from others harming me. I'm not going to lie, this is a real tough one. Probably *the* toughest one. It takes time and sometimes a lot of therapy to get through it. Sometimes when you think you have achieved forgiveness, something else comes along and rips open that wound again. Start over, keep trying, don't let this conquer you. Remember, this is for you and no one else, and you, my friend, are worth the effort.

Now it is your turn. If you could wave a magic wand and achieve forgiveness for another person's actions against you, what would that look like? Who would that be? And what would you forgive them for? Write that down here:

Now tell me, if you could wave a magic wand and achieve forgiveness for your own past actions against someone else or yourself, what would that look like? What specifically would you forgive yourself for? Write that down here:

Finally, how do you think you would feel if you achieved this forgiveness? Specifically, what feelings might you experience physically and emotionally if you achieved this forgiveness for yourself or another? Remember forgiveness is for you, not the other person. Write that down here:

_____

_____

_____

Letting go of fear is the second scene setter. As I mentioned earlier, fear can be debilitating. It is a powerful emotion that significantly impacts our actions. First, let me say that a good dose of fear can be a healthy thing, like when you are considering jumping out of an airplane, or admiring that cute little snake on your desert hike. Fear keeps us safe. We as humans are hard-wired to sniff out anything dangerous and avoid it. Evolutionarily speaking, this saved the human race. Back in the good ol' cave days, we were looking for those saber-toothed cats around every corner and being suspicious of those red berries on the bush, because they had the very real potential to nix us.

Fear serves a purpose indeed. However, in the 21st century, we really don't have too many saber-toothed cats lurking about and I know that the raspberries I purchase at the market are quite likely to be safe to eat by the fistful. Fear in 21st century living is more of a construct within our own minds than a minute-to-minute action definer as it was back in the day. Even though we are bombarded with horrific headlines every day, this literally is the safest time to live in human history. Now, I am not saying that you should rid yourself of all fear, as I have already established it can be a good thing to triple check that parachute, and to avoid doing the cha-cha with a rattlesnake. However, irrational fears get in the way of our life experiences and our ability to savor joyous moments.

Let me share an example with you of both success and failure in this realm. I have a ridiculous fear of heights, as many people do. Here is the thing: I really wanted to climb Camelback Mountain in Phoenix. Perhaps you might be thinking, come on Carrie, Camelback is not that tough of a climb, what the heck?! This isn't Everest, for crying out loud. Wait for it. I am a lover of hiking and being adventurous outdoors. I also like to make a "plan of action" so that I know exactly what to expect during my travel adventures. Well, I ended up watching too many YouTube videos of hikers on this mountain, some of whom came down bloodied and bruised, and reading too many articles warning of the daily rescue operations for those that "thought" they were a "good hiker" but ultimately . . . not so much. So going into the adventure, I was already a bit freaked out. I was hiking with my partner, who, by the way, also happens to be afraid of heights. We made our way up the mountain and as we went upward the crowds started to get thinner and thinner. Up, up we went, feeling cautiously optimistic about the whole endeavor. After careful footfalls and scrambling up rocks (while watching for those cute desert snakes), we got to a plateaued area with a beautiful view of the city. Feeling quite accomplished, we drank in the view, arms wrapped around each other, enjoying the beautiful moment. And then we realized we were nowhere near the summit. We watched with jaws agape as hikers were coming down a ledge to our left. OK, so we quickly realized that was the really easy part of the hike I had read about that we had accomplished; now it was getting real.

As we continued our climb upward, the trail was really not a trail anymore, but a series of colored dots painted on boulders pointing us in the right direction, almost like one of those old "choose your own adventure" story books, like if you pick the wrong path, there is a death ledge waiting for you. Already leery of the height issue, now we had an "I have no clue where I am going" issue. We got to a point where I had to wrap my arms around a large boulder and scootch my way around it to get to the other side to continue following the little dots. Unfortunately for us, I looked down at that point and saw death with no guard rail in between. The look on my face was enough for my partner to sit down and have an internal chat with himself. I quickly joined him. After several minutes of trying to psych ourselves up to scootching around this rock, we decided to take a photo of us "summiting" right there and quickly went back down the mountain, tails between our legs. What a defeating moment, and I still regret it to this day. Yes, fear is real, but it was also just in my head as an internal construct I had created that blocked me from accomplishing my goal. I saw some of the folks that were coming back down from the summit, and I am not tooting my own horn, but they looked more weary than I was at that moment. I know I could have done that summit and I should have done that summit. Physically I totally could climb the mountain; that was not the problem. My head got in the way of my legs. Now I have regret—but a good story to share about why it's important to let go of fear. And a good new goal to accomplish for when I return to Phoenix. Poor Camelback won't know what hit her when I fly back into town!

As promised, I also have a story to share about conquering fear, so I don't come off as a Negative Nellie for you folks. Here it goes. As you are quite aware by now, I have a healthy fear of heights. On a family vacation to Florida when my children were young, we ventured out to Gatorland! Yes folks, I know you are all mighty jealous of me at this point. It actually is a lovely park, so if you get the chance to go there, you won't be disappointed. Anyway, Gatorland has an opportunity for ziplining over the gator pits, so of course the kids wanted to do that. Never mind the fear of heights at this point, I was more concerned with being ripped to shreds by the rolling alligators beneath me. All I could think about was *Romancing the Stone* at this point—those of you that have never watched this classic, queue this one up in your Netflix binge list to appreciate the possibility of gators tearing you limb from limb and to see Michael Douglas sporting a white, unitard-like pantsuit.

I was feeling pretty darn proud of myself for getting through the ziplines, until it came to the last one. To get to said zipline, you needed to walk over this *Indiana Jones and the Temple of Doom* kind of rope bridge. There was absolutely no way I was getting across that bridge, so in front of everyone (including my kids), I had to do the walk of shame, down the stairs and around to the end of the ziplining fun with my feet firmly planted on the ground. Now maybe you are starting to wonder where the fear conquering is in this story. Here we go. Fast forward several years: my kids are much larger now and we are on a trip to Costa Rica. They got to choose the one adventure package we would do on that trip: yup, you guessed it, ziplining. The package was pretty cool actually; horseback riding up a volcano, ziplining down the mountain, and finishing with mud baths and bathing in geothermal springs. Did you see how they snuck that ziplining thing in the middle there?

So we traveled up the volcano mountainside on horseback with some precarious footings, but I was doing OK because I trusted my horse, knowing she probably did this about seven times a day. We got up to the top of the mountain where we had to wait forever in the rain to get all geared up, not enough workers that morning. . . . With the anxiety mounting, I was physically shaking from the cold and fear combo. We all lined up to start the ziplining and the employee asked who wanted to go first. Of course, my son jumped at the chance. Oh boy, not only did I have to do this, but I had to watch my first-born jump off the side of the mountain first. Off he went. I was terrified. I decide to go next, in between my son and my daughter. It wasn't like I could do anything, I was virtually incoherent at this point in time, but I thought it would be the correct parental thing to do. After the first line, my son asked if I saw the amazing waterfall. No—my eyes were closed, and I was too busy screaming for dear life to appreciate such natural beauty. After the second or third line I realized the fear was doing nothing for me, but everything to hurt me, and blunt my joy in this once-in-a-lifetime kind of situation. And like that, before I knew it, I was flying down the side of a mountain in Costa Rica. Teetering on little ledges they called "platforms" in between each line, huddled together like sardines with 12 other people I had just met, traversing line by line all the way down the mountain to mud bath bliss. Here's the fear conquering part. I hurtled my way down a mountain. In Costa Rica. Clipped to a wire. With a smile on my face and my eyes wide open. And had the realization that it was absolutely spectacular despite what I thought to be my impenetrable fear of heights. Fear is a negative emotion that just takes up space; we need to sweep that garbage off the stage and make way for more joy.

Your turn. What are you afraid of? What is holding you back from enjoying all of the glorious experiences life has to offer? Write that down here:

If you could wave that magic wand again and eliminate that fear, what would you do and how might you feel doing this?

Next we have self-compassion practice, which is a third grouping of stage setting activities to help build your behavior change success story. The self-compassion practice includes mindfulness, common humanity, and self-kindness. Picture this grouping coming together as a beautifully grilled burger, with pickles and onions on a sesame seed bun—but good for you. And the special sauce on top of that burger is gratitude. I will take you step by step through how to create this burger-eating experience. I want you to humor me and imagine that we are watching a lovely cooking show together, cooking up this masterpiece and incorporating it into your story line as the best darn dinner you have ever had.

The first component to self-compassion is mindfulness. Mindfulness is quite the buzzword these days. Toss a stone and you will find it in news articles, textbooks, movies, apps, marketing for hemp seeds, you name it. If I asked the general population what mindfulness is, I more than likely would receive the response of "living in the moment." And that would be partially correct! But is that all it is? My golden retriever Winn Dixie, who adores tennis balls, could also be described as living in the moment when I toss her a ball, yet she is not being mindful. So, what exactly is the difference between playing tennis with Winn Dixie and being mindful while you cook, eat, drive, or meditate? Well, living in the moment is the first element of mindfulness, and by this I mean checking in with that inner narrator once more and making sure you are not ruminating on past memories or fretting about future plans. It is being right here, right now, both in mind and in body, at this moment—then let that go for the next moment, and then let that one go for the next moment, and so on. You get the picture.

The second element of mindfulness is to be aware. So, as you relinquish your perseverating rear view mirror thoughts of the past and your incessant worrying and "to-do" listing for the future, soak up what your senses are telling you at that given moment. This awareness of the senses is an important skill in developing your mindfulness practice. Let me explain with an example. Let's say you are sitting on the patio enjoying a quiet hamburger dinner with your friend. Being mindful in this scenario would look like this:

- Smelling the burger before you start eating, as it triggers your hunger sensations and sets your stomach to growling and your mouth to watering.
- Tasting the burger, including each element of it (like the pickle, onion, and sesame seed bun), and how they all come together to offer you this unique taste.
- Feeling and acknowledging the sensations in your mouth and in swallowing it.
- Noting the sensations of feeling hunger in the beginning and feeling fullness toward the end of the meal.
- Feeling the sunshine on your face and its warmth on your body.
- Hearing the birds and squirrels chatter for a taste of that sesame seed bun.
- Listening keenly to your friend talk about how she learned how to cook this on her favorite cooking show app, including all her trials and tribulations with each step.
- Watching Winn Dixie gaze softly at you, hoping for sesame seed bun leftovers before the squirrels and birds get to them.
- Realizing your feet are on the ground, you are seated on your sits bones in your semi-comfortable patio chair, and your hands are holding a juicy burger.

After reading this list, think about the last meal you ate. Were you distracted by your phone, the TV, a needy toddler, a dog's hungry stares, filling in a crossword puzzle, or jotting down a shopping list of groceries you will need for tomorrow's dinner? Or were you really present and soaking up your senses' data surrounding you moment to moment? When was the last time you soaked up any experience using all your senses like this?

Once you can acknowledge what you are seeing, hearing, feeling, smelling, and tasting, and understanding where your body is in relation to the ground and space in any type of activity, that brings us to a mindfulness practice's final characteristic: accepting. And this is the hard part. It is great to be present and aware, but if you are judging experiences, pushing away things that bother you, or holding tight to those things that you enjoy, you are negating the process of mindfulness. Let me explain with the burger scenario once more.

Let's say you are enjoying this burger experience and you are having a lovely conversation with your friend when the neighbor's dog steals Winn Dixie's tennis ball and they start to bark and banter. And you think to yourself, "Ugh, I was having such a great time until I had to deal with all of this barking. I hate barking and it is ruining the dinner altogether." That is an example of pushing away what you are trying to be mindful and accepting of (the noise, the commotion, etc.) instead of being with this experience as it unfolds. By pushing away this experience and wishing it to go away, you are limiting your mindfulness practice, avoiding the present moment, and entering a negative space, wishing for future moments or reminiscing about past moments of no barking and a settled Winn Dixie. If, on the contrary, you are having such a lovely time you think to yourself, "Oh, I wish this moment would never end. I am having such a great time with my friend," here again, you are trying to cling to something that is impermanent. By dreaming of extending this into the future, you will not truly be in this moment and will be sad when the dinner ends instead of being appreciative in the moments you have together. Pleasant experiences and uncomfortable experiences alike both end because the only constant thing is change. Judging, holding on to, or avoiding experiences only serve to push you into the future or the past instead of living in and appreciating the moment. With each new experience coming to your senses, try to open to them as you would welcome an old friend. No judgment, no worries . . . just accepting them as they come to you.

The next component of self-compassion is common humanity. Common humanity simply means that we all screw up. We all burn the burger or forget to shake up the ketchup bottle, so we get that weird water stuff on our bun sometimes; no one can have a perfect burger every time. Common humanity is acknowledging that we all are imperfect; everyone is flawed, and that is OK. Suffering is a common human bond we all share with each other; messing up is what it means to "be human." By accepting our stumbles and being less judgmental about those times when we don't hit the mark, we can support a self-compassion practice, and in turn that helps us to be a kinder person to both ourselves and others. When we are kinder to ourselves and others, we bounce back from adversity more quickly, that is, have more resilience, and in turn lead a happier, more successful life.

Another way that I can describe resilience is to say that it is buoyancy of sorts, like popping back up above the water after doing a cannonball. Some folks are born with a strong characteristic of resilience, just like some kids are inherently able to float, throw a ball, play miniature golf, or run better than others. But just like working on the skills of learning how to float, throw a ball, play mini golf, or run better, you can learn how to be more resilient too. By viewing life's adversities as growing and learning opportunities, you can build your resilience skills. Remember our common humanity; we will all face adversity and problems, some big, some small. Intentionally building resilience can strengthen your adaptability to those problems. By harnessing these stage setting activities, you can build your resilience, but it takes effort and intention to do so.

The final characteristic of self-compassion is self-kindness. Remember, this is not Stuart Smalley stuff here. It is simply holding yourself in the same regard that you would a friend. Let's revisit our burger experience scenario. Say you went to your friend's house, and she tried to cook you this wonderful burger dinner that she learned how to make on the cooking show app. While grilling, the flames leapt upward and burned all the burgers, despite her best efforts to tend to them. She begins to cry and exclaims, "I can't even cook a Pop-Tart without burning it! Why did I ever think I could actually grill us a proper meal? I am just horrible at this!" Now think to yourself, what would you say to your friend? For real—specifically write down right here or say out loud what you would say to her:

If I had to hazard a guess, I would imagine you would say things like:

- It's OK, we can get takeout.
- I know you can do this; it was just a bad turn of luck that the grill flamed up.
- This same thing happened to me last week; no worries, it happens to everyone.
- I really just wanted to spend time with you. The burgers weren't that important to me.
- Do you want to start over? We can make them together!

I hazarded these guesses because I am certain you are a decent human being that has friends and enjoys spending time with them. You probably would put your arm around her, or you maybe even would have hugged her, too, you are that good of a person. So here is what I want you to think about right now. Switch places with your friend. If you would have burned the burgers, would you say these same things I listed above to yourself via your inner narrator? Or would you have judged yourself much more harshly by saying things like, "I am a screw up," or "I can't believe I did that," or "I am no good at cooking and I never will be, I should just give up," or "I don't know why I even try." So, if your inner narrator would have said things like this instead of the kind words you would offer to your friend, then I want you to brainstorm ideas on why you think that is and how you might be able to start flipping that switch from antagonist to protagonist.

Self-kindness is literally just treating yourself like you would treat your friend. In a recent conversation with a buddy of mine, I offered this same question. She was hurting from a past relationship, questioning her self-worth and her ability to be with someone that truly cares for her. She shared some of the thoughts that ran through her mind about why she felt her past relationship failed, all surrounding her perceived lack of positive characteristics in herself. In response, I asked her if she would say those things to or about me, since we both have "failed" past relationships. She was aghast. "Of course not!" Then I asked why she would say those things about herself. Next time you "mess up," turn the situation around and pretend it was your friend that "messed up." Set the stage to tell yourself those kind words of encouragement instead of allowing that inner jerk to take charge and rule your life.

A loving kindness meditation practice is one way you can support your work in the self-kindness arena. This practice basically just keeps a loving space for yourself. Despite the fear, anxiety, negativity, and generalized not-so-great stuff that happens in everyone's life, loving kindness offers you the space to take care of yourself in a quiet and calm way. It is a gentle barrier to shield you from your inner critic and, let's face it, all the other jerks out there, too. Loving kindness is the intention of wishing yourself well. Literally telling yourself that you wish to be safe, healthy, happy, and to live your life with some sort of comfort. When you hear the inner jerk creeping in, rebut that with, "May I be safe, and/or may I be healthy, and/or may I be happy, and/or may I live with kindness," or whatever quick and easy phrases have meaning and feel right to you. I know this might sound squishy, weird, and awkward, but it works. Give it a try the next time your Negative Nellie comes creeping around to try and ruin your show. On a side note, you can also throw this in reverse and send your intentions to someone else to support both your and your friend's well-being. If a friend or loved one is going through a difficult time, you can offer them loving kindness thoughts, too. Giving to others, or feeling like you are contributing to others' happiness, safety, and well-being, can make you feel better about a situation, too.

Let's do a check in. How often do you treat yourself like you would treat a friend?

- Never
- Sometimes
- Frequently
- Most Always

If you checked never or sometimes, why do you think that is?

_____
_____
_____
_____
_____

Gratitude is the special sauce on top of the self-compassion burger. Gratitude is being grateful for all of your blessings, even for those things you don't seem to see as blessings at the time. Recall the story about my panic attacks; I most certainly was not grateful for those, nor did I ever think I could believe them to be blessings, but looking back, I know that they were. They were the catalysts to start my awakening process. There are so many things to be grateful for, big and small; just take a moment to brainstorm. Brainstorm those blessings in the morning before you get out of bed, or at night as you are falling asleep, or anytime you have a spare 15 seconds in your day. Embracing a gratitude practice is a quick and easy intervention to set the stage for health and happiness.

Research shows us that being grateful can actually rewire our brains. As humans we tend to see the bad, the negative, the threats in life, and rightfully so, because this mechanism is in place to keep us safe—remember those cats and snakes. We are hard-wired for survival, not for happiness. Think about the last time you got a performance evaluation. There were probably far more pleasant things said in the evaluation than negative ones, but did you cling to the negative? Most do. Unfortunately, we tend to let the good in life pass us by (generally speaking) using this mindset. Embracing a gratitude practice steers us away from negativity and toward seeing the goodness that is abundant all around us.

An easy way to flip from a negative mindset to one of gratefulness is to stop apologizing and use the words "thank you" instead. Let me show you how this works. You are late to a meeting with your colleagues because you stopped to help someone find their way to a conference room in a different part of the building. When you arrive at your meeting, instead of saying, "Sorry I am running behind," flip that apology into gratitude by saying, "Thank you for waiting for me, I was helping someone else and got a bit behind." Or when you are unable to attend your nephew's soccer match, say, "Thank you for understanding my time constraints" instead of "I'm sorry I can't come to the pitch on Saturday." Even if we are not totally embracing a gratitude practice at the outset of the journey, simply acknowledging that you do have things to be grateful for supports this shift in perspective. Just minor little changes in our behaviors help us rewire our brains to set the stage for happiness and health. Employing a gratitude practice can actually rewire our brains over time to see more positive than negative, which in turn helps us to be happier, less depressed, and less anxious. But again, it must be done with intent and must be practiced as much as you would practice your golf swing or your yoga poses. So, at the end of that lovely burger dinner with your friend, be sure to share your gratitude with her. It will support both of your health and wellness journeys.

Now I would like you to write down ten things you are grateful for, right here, right now. But here's the catch: they can't be big things like family, children, your partner, or your parents. Rather, write down the little things, those daily blessings that so often go overlooked. I will start you out. Here are just some of the things I am grateful for at any given moment of the day: laughter, my heated blanket, sunsets, a tandem Downward Dog pose with my dog, learning new information, the way my Chacos perfectly fit my feet and have purple little flowers on them, holding hands, dark chocolate, photo memories that randomly pop up on my phone, stretchy pants, hugging trees, wool socks, hugging people, making new friends, kindly neighbors, a functioning dishwasher, heated car seats, and crunchy peanut butter. That was way more than ten, sorry, I get pretty excited about this stuff! Now it's your turn. Write down the first ten things that you are grateful for, right here, right now, then think about how you feel and what your inner narrator is saying right after you write those down. Remember that feeling; it will help you make this a regular practice.

What I am grateful for:

How I feel right now after thinking about what I am grateful for:

Let's take a final moment before we move away from the self-compassion practices conversation to distinguish the difference between self-esteem and self-compassion. Perhaps you may be thinking that these activities are all to support your self-esteem. Well, they're not. Surprised? Self-esteem is a fickle friend and one that, I feel, has gotten us into the cyclical problem of poor resiliency and fear of trying to be a better version of ourselves. In today's society, we give every kid a medal for participation, we treat ourselves with a Dilly Bar for passing an exam, and yearn for a digital badge for simply attempting a wellness journey stepping stone. These sorts of extrinsic motivators can support self-esteem and perhaps Stuart Smalley's ridiculous self-validations, but they do not support self-compassion or self-confidence. Self-esteem is there for you when you win a competition, make your weight loss goal, or score higher than your buddy on an exam. But when you don't achieve those things, self-esteem is nowhere to be seen, and you are left feeling not so great about yourself. Self-compassion offers a sense of understanding with gains and losses; it rejoices in our uniqueness, offers a growth mindset perspective to challenges and stumbles, and gives us a space for personal healing. It is there for you during both successes and failures, and helps you to rebound faster when you inevitably encounter those stumbles and struggles in life.

Finding joy is the fourth, final, and (I think) one of the most fun stage setting activities! Deliberately seeking out the joyous pleasures in life support all of these other activities. It goes hand in hand with a gratitude practice because it can rewire our brains to be a happier version of ourselves. Finding joy with intention to deliberately see the good in people, situations, and ourselves is a positive feedback loop; the more you do it with intent, the less intention and effort you will have to muster for future joy-finding missions. One time many years ago when I was walking into work, a random lady stopped me on the street and said, "You look so joyous!" Honestly, this is one of the best compliments I have ever received in my life. First, she took the time to really be mindful and observant of everything happening around her, and second, she took the time to share this beautiful compliment with me. I wish I knew who she was so that I might thank her and share how impactful that moment in time was for me. The point is, I was walking into work. Not many people would probably think that was a joyous moment in life, but at the time, I was really happy to have a job that I loved and felt like I was making a difference. And that joy showed from the inside out, and then spread a little happiness to people along the way and to those around me.

Stop and think about what things and activities make you joyous, what joy looks like in you and radiating outward from you, and how that affects those around you. Write those ideas down here:

Now think about how often you engage in these things you just listed. Is it as often as you like? If not, why not? What can you change in your everyday life to find more joy? Look back to your list of things you are grateful for. Do those also bring you joy? Yes! These concepts are all interrelated! Can you find joy in other things? Smaller things? Like seeing a butterfly, appreciating that your teenager put her dishes in the dishwasher without being told, or getting a doggo kiss in your ear while doing your morning sit-ups? Find those small joyous moments and cherish them, rejoice in them, and share your joy with others by letting it radiate outward. Emotions are contagious—all emotions—so think about what emotions you currently are surrounded by and what emotions you would like to share with others in the world.

The show must go on!

Now that we have set our stage, we can begin the auditioning process for all of the supporting roles in our lives. Social connectedness is a huge influence on our wellness journey. Ever notice that when your friends and family are making suspect choices, you are more likely to follow along with the same types of choices? Or when your friends are making more positive healthy choices, you are more likely to do that, too? Well, there is a reason for that. In the next chapter, let's explore this notion and get a better idea of who should be on stage with you in those supporting roles.

CHAPTER FOUR

SUPPORTING ACTORS IN YOUR STORY

Now that you know who the main character and narrator for your story are and have the tools to set your scene so that you can be the best version of yourself that you can be, it is up to you to choose your supporting actors. This process must be done wisely and with care. It is an important build up in the story line of your wellness journey, because surrounding yourself with the right people will support strong character development and healthy living choices for yourself. In turn, it also allows you the opportunity to be a strong supporting actor to others in their journey by way of strengthening relationships, role modeling positive behaviors, and offering supportive words of encouragement. What would Dorothy be without the Tinman, Scarecrow, and Lion? Certainly not as appreciative of home, family, and friends to help stave off sadness, loneliness, and fear. And where would they all be without her? Certainly not as brainy, stuffed, or buffed. There is a vast audience watching your story, and you are a supporting actor in so many others' stories too; we are all interdependent in each other's character development and unfolding plots!

Your supporting actors include your family, children, partner, friends, neighbors, co-workers, community members . . . the list goes on and on! Basically everyone you come into contact with. Wrapping ourselves in positive social connectedness greatly impacts our health and well-being. For this chapter I am going to use the analogy of Russian nesting dolls (Hayden, 2019) to highlight the importance of a theoretical health model when considering behavior change throughout your wellness journey. Not to worry! I promise to not bore you to tears with theoretical underpinnings to behavior change. Alas, I have not tricked you into reading a textbook here (surprise, Chapter Four is for all you grad students out there!). Just kidding, this book is all about fun storytelling, so let's take this one little baby matryoshka doll at a time.

But first we need to take a closer look at what a healthy relationship actually entails before we start going through auditions for supporting actor roles.

If you want to find great relationship advice, just look at social media; there are a million different quizzes out there to determine who your best mate would be. There seems to be a very strong correlation between matchmaking and finding a perfect life mate based on which character on *Game of Thrones* you would be (pretty sure mine is Daenerys). Please note I am just kidding—there is no way I am being serious here. Honestly speaking, though, there are certain characteristics that are inherent in healthy relationships. Looking for these characteristics should be on your checklist during the auditioning process. Some of these may seem ridiculously simple, total no-brainer kinds of things, but just like that inner critic we all have, some folks can be slippery and sneaky in their unhealthy interactions with you. Trust me, you do not want an understudy that is pining for your lead role, just waiting for you to make a blooper only to swoop in and swipe that role from you or to turn the audience against you. I am certain we have all been duped by someone like this at some point in our lives. Speaking from experience, I tend to look at the bright side of most things and give most people the benefit of a doubt, but naivety can be a weakness and cause pain sometimes, so it's always best to exercise a wee bit of caution.

The first and most important characteristic in any type of relationship is safety. I know, it sort of goes without saying, but how many times have you put yourself in a position of being hurt in order to help another person, be it a friend, relative, or partner? Don't get me wrong, altruism is beautiful, but not at the cost of your safety. Being a nurse, I like to help others, but if I am hurt and unwell, that prevents me from helping others. It is like the airline attendant telling parents to put the oxygen mask on themselves first. We all want to keep those we care about safe from harm and do whatever we can to help them, but first things first, you need to help yourself to be of help to others. In any kind of relationship, you need to be safe, and that doesn't mean just physically safe, but emotionally, mentally, spiritually, socially, and financially safe. Don't forget about yourself as a potential antagonist here, too. Remember that inner critic? That little jerk is not safe for you. Remember that self-compassion meditation practice we talked about earlier? The very first phrase that I offered to you is "may I be safe". That is the foundation in any relationship, including the relationship you have with yourself. Without safety there is no real relationship; it is simply a power grab shell game, and no one will walk away from that whole or healthy.

In any relationship you can fall into one of three categories: victim, survivor, or thriver. Clearly, we all want all of our relationships to fall into that thriver category. We should seek to engage in relationships that support our happiness and successes in life, surrounding ourselves with those that rejoice in our triumphs and are there for us when we falter. An example statement from a thriver could be someone saying, "Man, I love being with you, we travel so well together and I always have the best time just hanging out with you." The survivor category is making do with a not-so-great situation. This might be the difficult boss at work that we can't seem to shake until we find a different job, or they leave their current role, or some other aspect of the relationship shifts in one direction or another. The situation is not ideal, but we manage to at least try to have a positive outlook, employ workarounds, and find a way to participate in the relationship without significant damage to our health. An example statement from someone in a survivor role could be, "I know we don't really get along most of the time, but I can appreciate your attention to detail in event planning and hopefully you can appreciate my talents in finding the best in a situation." Finally, there is the victim role. If safety is a concern in the relationship, more often than not you will fall into the victim role, either knowingly or not. When you function in this role you are caught in a cycle of fear, self-doubt, and potentially even self-loathing, which results in cyclical unhappiness and poor health. A statement by someone in the victim role could look something like this: "She is so mean to me all the time but there is nothing I can do to change that; I just have to keep my head down and hope she doesn't get angry with me." It is good to take stock of where your relationships lie in this arena and reflect on what is helping you versus hurting you.

Pause for a moment to take stock of your relationships.

- Are you predominantly in the thriver or survivor role?
- Do you function in the victim role in any of your relationships?

Hit the pause button to determine who your support people are and who or what relationships might be harming your health. Don't forget to reflect on a self-assessment here as well.

- What was the outcome of listening to your inner narrator previously?
- Is your relationship with yourself in the thriver, survivor, or victim role?

Respect is next in the lineup of healthy relationship characteristics. It sort of goes hand in hand with safety and the thriver, survivor, victim roles, but respect takes it one step further. If you have respect for yourself and others, you will have a safe space in which you can freely share ideas, thoughts, and feelings, all within healthy boundaries. But here's the step further: without judgment. Respect is honoring an individual's autonomy and being considerate of their thoughts and feelings. Everyone deserves to be heard and have a space for sharing inner reflections. Can you be open, honest, and vulnerable with this person (or yourself) and still feel safe? If the answer is yes, then you have that person's (or self) respect.

Support is next in the queue. Support can look like that special someone that is a cheerleader for you, or even that person that is just simply present, aware of, and responsive to your needs, like the understudy waiting patiently in the wings to help you with your line if you happen to forget it. Now being a supportive cheerleader does not mean you need that special someone to tell you that your ex is completely to blame, or that your boss is a complete and utter cottonheaded ninnymuggins (although that does feel good sometimes), but this support person will also need to call out your rubbish when rubbish happens. It is never just one person's fault, and your boss may be a cottonheaded ninnymuggins but still might have some value in the feedback she is giving you. Also, remember common humanity? We all muck stuff up, and our support actors are there for us when we do, unconditionally. But support in action should look like that arm wrapped around you telling you that yeah, you might have bungled the job, but at the same time point out all of the good that you have done and will still do based on the hard life lesson you just learned. Think about who in your life can pick you up, help you dust yourself off, and take that next big courageous step after a stumble. That is what support looks like in a healthy relationship.

Write down who that person or those people are:

_____

_____

_____

It's not my way or the highway in a healthy relationship; you need compromise to stay healthy. Compromise means that you can at least see something from another's perspective. No one will agree with another human being 100% of the time. No one should get their way 100% of the time; that would be completely unfair, unbalanced, and unhealthy. By giving a little, you actually get a lot. You can have the opportunity to support each other in being heard and respected by creating a safe space to connect. In doing so, you can learn how to do things a different way that may even work out better than your way! I always joke that "the world according to Carrie Jarosinski would be a pretty great place," but in reality, it would be pretty lousy. By giving in, bending, and coming together via compromise, we can always make something that's already good, great.

Finally, we need to be able to communicate with each other in a caring space. Communication that is open and honest without being hurtful is another keystone in healthy relationships. Talking about feelings and difficult topics with a reasoned awareness of others' feelings and respecting boundaries by avoiding yelling or angry confrontation are appropriate means of verbal communication. That is kind of a given and something we should have learned from *Sesame Street*; unfortunately, it doesn't happen as often as it should. Don't believe me? Just watch political debates or what happens when someone has to wait in line too long at the airport.

Keep in mind that communication isn't just about verbal communication; you need to be aware of those nonverbals too. Think about all of the ways humans communicate with each other aside from our words, such as physical spacing, eye contact, facial expressions, body movements. These are hugely impactful and important to supporting healthy communication in relationships. Keep in mind how those nonverbals may or may not align with the verbal communication you are offering or being offered in your interactions. If someone is telling you that they respect and support you and your safety, yet begin playing on their phone when you start talking about your challenging day at work, or have a bumper sticker on their car that reads "Horn broken watch for finger," they may not be the best communicator or the best choice of supporting actor for you.

The flip side of communicating your thoughts and feelings is listening. Active listening to actually hear what the person is saying is a critical element of the communication process. That means when another person is talking, you are not thinking about your response or your emotional reaction to what they are saying, or reminiscing about how burned the grilled burger was that your friend made for you the other night. You are there in that moment being heard while you are speaking, and actively listening while the other person is speaking, and offering your nonverbal cues. It is a two-way street that all too often can become a one-way dead-end road with a roundabout that neither person can escape when caring communication breaks down.

There are many other characteristics of healthy relationships that I will not belabor because most of those directly coincide with those that are already listed here (characteristics such as honesty, integrity, individuality, kindness, empathy, trust, etc.), so we will stick to these basics for right now. Later on, we will investigate your values and how they align with healthy relationship characteristics to give you a deeper appreciation of what your ideal relationships should demonstrate in order to support your own personal health and well-being. But for now, we are all clear on what the basic characteristics of healthy relationships look like, so we can start to analyze the different layers of those supporting actors in your life.

Looking at the Russian nesting doll analogy, I want you to imagine the very first doll, the teeny tiny baby doll in the middle. Most often this is just one solid piece of wood that the artist has carved and painted. This is you, whole and beautiful and strong!

For the first exercise in this chapter, we will start analyzing those characteristics in this first doll, aka yourself. Looking back on all that we have discovered so far in this book about you, how would you rate yourself on a scale of 1 to 4 in these characteristics? 1 is "I really need to have a chat with Big Bird and his neighborhood friends about the basics of how to be kind right about now," and four is "I am the Dalai Lama." Seriously though, I want you to quantify how your relationship is with yourself in these areas. Here we go with our own social media quiz (sorry, no *Game of Thrones* characters in this one!):

Safety

I have my inner antagonist in check and under control.

1   2   3   4

I am a thriver in most of my inner narrations.

1   2   3   4

Respect

I can be real with myself about my feelings, thoughts, and ideas.

1   2   3   4

I can be vulnerable with these ideas and still feel safe at the same time.

1   2   3   4

Support

I understand that when I mess things up, I have the capability of picking myself up and learning from my mistakes.

1   2   3   4

I treat myself as I would treat a friend when I falter.

1   2   3   4

Compromise

I seek out alternate ideas and incorporate some of those into my life.

1   2   3   4

I understand that I do not have to have everything my way all of the time.

1   2   3   4

> ### Communication
>
> I am open and honest with myself without being hurtful.
>
> 1 2 3 4
>
> I am mindful of my thoughts and feelings.
>
> 1 2 3 4

This quick little check in will give you a better understanding of what your attitudes and beliefs are in regard to your personal relationship with yourself, otherwise known as your intrapersonal relationship. There are no right or wrong answers here, no median score to tell you if you are healthy or not, no perfect *Game of Thrones* life partner character match based on your choices. Remember, this book is not a prescribed "diet plan to lose 20 pounds," "31 days to a flatter stomach," or a "meditate your way to enlightenment" kind of tool. This is simply an opportunity for you to take a temperature of where you are at right now and possibly serve as a means to setting a goal for yourself to work toward when you are ready. Keep in mind, though, that the closer you are to the Dalai Lama on this scale, the better the position you will be in.

Each move outward from the first nesting doll wraps you up in the beautifully painted hard shell of the next doll. Each of the nesting dolls that we will discuss in this chapter can serve to paint your world a beautiful color and also keep you safe from harm, just as healthy relationships can bring beauty, safety, and ultimately health to your life. Holding each of the dolls in a sacred space by choosing and maintaining healthy and strong relationships will ultimately help to keep you well. Without these nesting dolls or healthy relationships, your life will be a little less beautiful, less safe, and less healthy. A favorite saying of mine is "you reap what you sow"; in this example, that means that if you invest in safe supportive relationships, you will reap the rewards of them (and there are plenty of rewards, which we will talk about in a minute!). But if you do not take the time to invest your energy into building healthy and meaningful relationships, your health will suffer. It is the same as the type of energy that you put into this world and share with others. If you sow positivity, joy, and laughter, that is what you will reap, my friends! If you sow negativity, anger, and divisiveness, this too will be your harvest in the quality of your relationships, your health, and your life.

The second doll that wraps itself around you are interpersonal relationships. We will begin with those that are representative of your first family relationships, including your parents, sisters, brothers, and maybe your grandparents and cousins, depending upon your family structure. When I talk about familial relationships, those can mean biological family members like the mother that gave birth to you and the father that helped to create you with his genetic material, adoptive parents in the legal sense, foster parents, or those parental figures that you informally adopted into your life. Basically, those that helped to raise you into the human you are right now (this may be one, a combination of some, or all of these types of folks). Same thing goes with those sisters and brothers, grandparents, and cousins in your life. Those can be the relations that you are biologically connected to, those you were raised with, or those you happily stumbled upon in life one way or another that serve in this familial role; again, they can be one or a combination of some or all of these types of people. These folks often will offer the strongest type of relationship; they offer bonding in your life and can be the most influential, since they are with you during those all-important developmental years when your brain is growing and changing, and you are learning about how relationships actually work. In theory, this should be the safe space where you are first introduced to relationship building, which allows you to grow and flourish and learn how to love. These relationships most often are long lasting and tenacious, there for you in the good, bad, and boring times.

I was lucky enough to be born into a very typical nuclear family that for the most part was normal (or at least that is what I think it is!). I have a mother, father, and two older brothers. I grew up in rural America and lived in a middle-class household. The relationships with my parents and siblings are healthy and strong. What makes them strong? Well, lots of things, but let me share a story about how I came to be while reflecting back on those characteristics we talked about earlier to highlight my point.

There is quite a bit of an age difference between myself and my brothers. I was one of those whoopsy-daisy kind of babies that happened with the latest and greatest spermicidal foam contraceptive that was all the rage back in the 70s. It was probably a pretty upsetting time for my parents. My mom was not supposed to get pregnant because she had a medical condition that placed her at great risk. My dad was the sole provider, they lived in a two-bedroom house, and my two older brothers were "all boy," so I am making just a small leap here in thinking my parents had a bit of a diarrhea moment when they found out about yours truly.

However, there was never any shame in this; no one tried to "hide" this story, nor was I ever treated like I was the red-headed stepchild that came barging into their lives with utter disruption. This was a story that was shared with me and anyone else who cared to listen throughout the years; it was never treated like a big, shameful secret that needed to be covered up. The story that was shared included a rational explanation of what happened, followed with much love in the way of "but you were the best surprise ever," and "we wouldn't have had a doctor in the family had you not shown up," and "you are my favorite daughter" kind of stuff. The story is part of who I am and why I am the way I am (good or bad I guess). But more importantly, it characterizes those healthy components of a relationship like good communication (sharing the story without hesitation), a safe space without judgment to talk about weird things that happened (like my parents having sex and having an oopsie-daisy kind of kid), compromise (as I wore boy hand-me-downs and caught frogs to be like one of the boys), support (everyone involved accepted the barn cats being dressed up in doll clothes and acted like that was a great accomplishment for me), respect for each other (no, she's not an only child, just the bumper crop and all is good), and love. My parents championed me during my childhood, most often behind the scenes, since it was before helicopter parenting was cool. Like when I sat the bench all summer season during softball one year and my mom gave a big earful to the coach without me knowing it (I really was quite awful though), or when my dad quietly tolerated my loud teenage "I can't stand you" years, or when my brothers carted me to dance lessons in the family truckster even when they had better things to do. We all came together through repeated daily interactions that demonstrated these characteristics in one way or another, and that supports and serves as a foundation for a healthy transition to adulthood. I am definitely not saying we were or are the perfect Partridge family; there was quite a bit of looney tunes going on in that farmhouse, but compared to most upbringings in the world, it was pretty darn good.

Now, I am not so naive to think that everyone had such a mundane, generic, American pie childhood such as I did. Some of you may be thinking, "I had a messed up, weird childhood, like the weird blond bob haircut He-Man had kind of weird," or even *Monty Python and the Holy Grail*-level weird. Still others had downright lousy, horrible childhoods, far beyond just weird stuff. I completely understand and appreciate that there are many who were not so blessed as I was.

There are these things called adverse childhood experiences, otherwise known as ACEs. ACEs can include experiences defined under three umbrella items, including child abuse, neglect, and household dysfunction. Abuse and neglect are pretty self-explanatory, but household dysfunction might need a bit more definition. These are things such as divorce, household mental illness, substance use disorders, an incarcerated family member, or a caregiver being treated violently. These experiences tend to form an intergenerational pattern, meaning if you experience this yourself, then your children are more likely to experience this also, and so the cycle repeats itself. Data on these range, but to give you some perspective, anywhere from one- to two-thirds of people in the general population experience at least one ACE, and the more ACEs experienced, the greater the negative health impacts. ACEs disproportionately affect women, minorities, and those with economic hardships. The health impacts of ACEs are many and can be lifelong. They include mental illness, physical illnesses, including cardiovascular disease and obesity, and lifestyle "choices" such as heavy drinking, smoking, and drug use. Just to give you a quick overview of the national impact of ACEs, according to the CDC (2022), one in six adults experiences four or more types of ACEs, five of the top ten leading causes of death are associated with ACEs, and preventing ACEs could lead to a 44% decrease in depression. As you can see, ACEs are pretty darn impactful across the lifespan to our health and well-being. In addition to all of these struggles, the relationships that are so critical to development and to learning about what a healthy relationship looks like are impaired for those that experience ACEs.

Let's pause and take some time to complete the ACEs quiz. Please note that this is not a comprehensive tool. It is just a brief quiz to identify if you are at a higher risk of certain challenges or health concerns based on your childhood exposures. It by all means does not predict your future. Also keep in mind that by embracing the wellness practices in this book, you can insulate yourself from any potential risks ACEs may pose.

To access the ACEs quiz, scan the QR code with your phone or type bit.ly/3PiDH6e into your browser.

Now, I am not saying that if you have experienced ACEs in your life that you are doomed to unhealthy relationships forever and ever, or an unhealthy life generally speaking. Clearly you are interested in living a healthier life, which is why you are here with me right now. This is where all of those important supporting actors come into play that might not be in the biological category of your storyline. While you cannot choose your family, you can choose who plays vital roles in your life. It could be the friendly neighbor that cared for you like a grandma, or the teacher that helped coach you through Little League all those years. It could be anyone who played and continues to play an important role in your daily relationships right now by consistently displaying those characteristics we talked about earlier. Sometimes this level of relationship just can't be filled with those traditional familial connections, so we seek out the even better substitutes (I like to call them the unicorns), and we need to hold on tight. These are the sisters from another mister and the brothers from another mother, and they are super duper important!

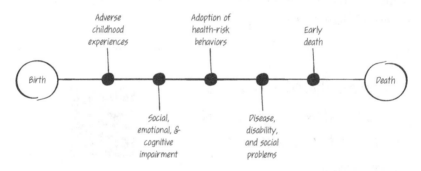

Relationship between early childhood trauma and health and well-being problems later in life.

Source: World Health Organization

Another component of this second Russian doll is close friends and partners. As we transition into adulthood, partners can supplement that familial role we talked about already, and should have those same healthy relationship characteristics. Sometimes these close friends and partners are the ones that step into the relationship vacuum if our childhood familial relationships are not as healthy as we would have liked. Even friends that might not be physically readily available at the drop of a hat for you could fill this need. There is something to be said about those friends that you might not chat with for weeks, months, or maybe even years, and then you meet up and just pick right back up where you left off.

Your partner, physically close friends, and not-so-physically-close close friends are your people, what I lovingly term your unicorns, those bonding relationship folks that you need in your life throughout adulthood to support your health and happiness. And just like I described earlier, they need you, too; you are their supporting actors in their story, just as they are in yours. Let me share some examples of my unicorns to give you an idea of what these relationships can look like in action. When I was going through a difficult time, one of these unicorns Snapped me every day just to check in and see how I was doing. Yes, we would walk and talk together when we could, but most days we couldn't physically see each other, so she Snapped me, sometimes just stupid random bitmojis to make me laugh, and other times a simple "Hey, how's it going?" She knew exactly the right amount and type of support I needed to get through the rough patch. So, when a friend of mine was in a tough spot, I took that love that I was given and paid it forward, doing the same thing for her. It's nice to know someone is thinking about you and has your back, even if it is just a silly bitmoji of you in a bunny costume asking what's up through Snapchat.

I have another friend that I literally have been connected to since preschool. We met at our moms' homemaker's meeting (more on the old neighborhood in a bit). I might not talk to this person for months, but you know what, if something happens, all I have to do is make one phone call and say, "I'm not so good," and she drops everything to help me work through it, share the burden of my pain, be my cheerleader support person, and just be there for me without judgment.

Once a year I take a "girls' trip." Me and the unicorns pile into a plane, irritate everyone around us with our insatiable laughter and ridiculous behavior, and just spend a wee bit of adult time together. That kind of unadulterated, fun-loving, not-a-care-in-the-world kind of unplugged fun. We don't have to talk on the phone every day, but when we get to that airport, we pick right back up where we left off. We offer each other that safe space to grumble about our "real life," rejoice in our successes, cheerleader when we stumble, and just overall be what we all need at any given moment.

You may be wondering, what about social media? Can I connect with my herd of unicorns there? You bet! Whatever you can do to stay connected to your people is important and makes a difference. I have friends from Germany that I see once every few years. Without social media, I never would have stayed connected to them. With social media, we can slide back into our friendship all "easy-peasy like" when we do finally get a chance to see each other again, because we have stayed connected. We watch each other's children grow and achieve milestones and enjoy some much-needed reconnection time through Facebook, Insta, and WhatsApp. I have a group of friends from high school, and we share an Instant Message group chat. We literally just communicate with each other through memes, and it is hysterical. Just about daily we are interacting with each other, stoking those old inside jokes and poking fun at some of the dumpster fires we have lived through in our lives. It literally just takes a moment of time, but it communicates "Hey, I'm thinking about you and wanted to brighten your day a little bit." I share these examples with you so that you can see that your herd of unicorns can and will look different in action from person to person, but know that however your herd acts or whoever your herd includes, they can support your well-being and your endeavors in any type of health behavior change. A herd can be just you and one other unicorn, or it can be a full-fledged rodeo; however, please note that quality always supersedes quantity. Take the time and effort to cultivate solid, sustainable, healthy relationships that demonstrate the characteristics we talked about earlier. These types of relationships are invaluable for the soul.

So how can you pivot from unhealthy interpersonal relationships to healthy ones? You will need to find people in your life that support you, your goals, and your health; those people that demonstrate safety, respect, support, compromise, and positive communication in your interactions and that align with your values. These unicorns will impact all aspects of your health and well-being. Find them and hold on tight to them. Biology doesn't matter; your unicorns do. And when you do find them, you need to be sure that you are a unicorn right back; they need you too.

The harder part will be to step back from those folks that are not so supportive of your health and well-being—those who do not offer you a safe space to just be you. The people who lack the respect of being mindful of your boundaries. Those who would rather put you down instead of raising you up. Those who are indifferent to your pain or are jealous of your success. The people who are all or nothing, black or white, who refuse to give and take or to see situations from a different perspective other than their own, and those that verbally or nonverbally communicate with you through anger, contempt, or apathy.

I keep talking about how these bonding relationships support your health, and you're probably thinking, what does that really mean? I mean, I know that having good friends makes me feel good, but come on, can it really make me a healthier human? Short answer: a resounding YES! Before we get into the nitty gritty of what health actually is (sorry, you have to wait for the next chapter for that goodness), let me just take a moment to share with you all of the healthy side effects of having unicorns in your life. Healthy relationships increase your happiness and reduce stress; they help you be more resilient and cope better with current, future, and past traumas; the reciprocal relationship dynamic can improve your own self-worth by offering you a sense of belonging and purpose; and healthy relationships can harness positive peer pressure to avoid slipping into negative habits like drinking too much and moving too little. These are great things for all aspects of health!

Before we move on, jot down who your unicorns are. Who can you rely on to help you when the chips are down or laugh with you when life is great? Write this down now.

My unicorns are:

_____

_____

_____

The next of the Russian nesting dolls are those folks that you come into contact with on a somewhat regular basis, but don't necessarily share your inner feelings and thoughts or share a unicorn status closeness with. These are your co-workers and supervisors, parents of your kids' friends, the bus driver on your regular route to work, your neighbors, fellow churchgoers, your partner's buddies, Pilates classmates, your local barista, volunteer mates . . . the list goes on and on. While these folks are not as impactful as those familial relationships and unicorns, they are still supportive of your health through social connectedness. These folks help you to feel as though you are supported through community connection. If I had to bring in an analogy here, it would be the Tree of Souls from the *Avatar* movie (not the kid movie, but the big blue CG alien *Avatar* movie). This tree represented the relationships, energy, and life force of the entire community, and signified the importance of that interconnectedness for everyone to prosper. Feeling as though you are a part of a larger whole is an integral part of staying engaged and connected to humanity. As we take a step further back from those close, interpersonal relationships that we discussed earlier and look at just social connectedness, we see even more health effects, such as reducing chronic disease like high blood pressure, staving off depression, and keeping your waistline in check.

Evolutionarily speaking, we were meant to be social critters, to laugh, share stories, make eye contact, connect, and engage with other humans in proximity to us. I recently watched a Rick Steves episode (he is an amazing PBS travel show guide who offers you some great educational travel experiences without leaving your couch) on traveling to Iran and something he said struck a chord about the importance of human connectedness. He shared that it is really difficult to drop bombs on people you know and like. Well, that pretty much sums this stuff up. In his travels to Iran, he met a young, college-aged woman out and about, and engaged in a conversation with her. She shared that Iranians love Americans! It was just our governments that didn't like each other. Wait, what?!? When you can connect with another human being one on one, chat, make eye contact, and engage in that human connection, life is happier, healthier, safer, better, and most often we evolve into nicer people because of that social connectedness. Now, I am not saying we will achieve world peace by chatting with folks in the neighborhood, but I am saying that just making connections with other human beings can sometimes bring down barriers that may have felt otherwise insurmountable. Thanks, Rick Steves, for being such a great ambassador for humanity. Let me share a few more examples on why these loose relationships of social connectedness are so important.

Think about where you live right now and where you have lived in the past. Do you have an affinity for one location over another? If so, it is more than likely due to the relationships and the level of engagement that surrounded you in that particular community. I have lived in the city, in the suburbs, and in the country at different points in my life. I feel most connected and happy living in the city, where I can walk down my street and run into all of my neighbors, chat a while, even if it is just idle prattle about the weather, and smile contentedly in recognition of those that walk past in my neighborhood that are a part of my life as I am going on my daily walks. Now this is quite strange, because I absolutely love the country. I am a tree hugger through and through. I love cows and chickens, I love connecting with nature, rubbing my bare feet in the grass, and I love the quiet of the countryside. However, in terms of my happiness, I am better suited living in the city, where I can feel this social connectedness on a regular basis.

You may recall that I also have the lived experience of growing up in the country. This was a pretty great experience as well, because we had amazing neighbors. Yes, we were very spread out and far away from each other (like get in the car because you have to drive to go see your neighbors kind of distance), but we knew them, celebrated with them, and loved them. The neighborhood would get together for "jam sessions" where anyone who wanted to could come together to make some pretty fun music, be it on the drums, guitar, or accordion. It didn't matter if you were young or old, what family you came from, or what kind of talent you had, we just came together as one to enjoy each other's company and celebrate life with a Jolly Good soda. And to this day, I still stay in contact with these neighbors. They serve as adoptive parents for me and grandparents for my kids. I stay connected with their kids and their grandkids on social media. It is pretty amazing, and it strengthens my health.

Conversely, I will share a story that depicts the impacts of these community-level relationships when they are not so good. Sorry to bring Negative Nellie back into this lovely discussion we are having, but sometimes it helps to hear about the bad so we can appreciate the good (common humanity, anyone?). In one of my jobs, I had a supervisor who was pretty horrible. Not, like, incompetent horrible, but just not supportive of me or my work, and at times simply demeaning to me, both behind closed doors and in larger group settings. I was pretty young and really did not have the first clue in how to deal with this. The relationship most certainly did not have the characteristics we talked about; quite the opposite. This relationship was so negatively impacting that I would feel horrible going to work, cry when I got home from work, and in turn hurt other relationships in my life because I was not happy or well. Now this person was not a unicorn (obviously), and was considered to be "only" a community-level type relationship, but it hurt my health and well-being drastically, and this was just one person! I am sure many of you out there can relate to such a story, be it a supervisor, a co-worker, a parent on the snack committee, you name it . . . we have all had to deal with a person we just can't groove with at one time or another. You can see how just one relationship can spill over into other areas of your life, right? Just as healthy relationships can help you to be happy and well, hurtful relationships can make you sad and sick. They are not worth it. Change the dynamic, walk away, cut the baloney out of your life and be a better person for it. Life is too short to waste time on someone that makes you unhappy and unhealthy.

Ever meet someone that you felt a connection with from the start? Like, man, I knew you in another time and I just know we had a great life together. I recently experienced this with an acupuncturist I met. I was going to my chiropractor, and he asked if I would ever consider acupuncture therapy. I was a bit hesitant, but this was not the first time it was brought up to me; my previous chiropractor had suggested the same thing. So, thinking the universe must be telling me something, I said, "Sure, why not, let's give this a try." In taking that leap of faith, I met this wonderful lady that not only made me feel better physically, but truly helped me on a holistic exploration of my spiritual and emotional wellness, something I was definitely not in the business of looking to work on at that moment. But there was a connection there, meaning I knew she was meant to be in my life at that moment and she felt the same about me. She helped me in my wellness journey in a space where I didn't realize needed help, and I helped her make connections to her new community. We picked up where we left off in that past life, as our lives intersected in this moment in time. Now, we are not going to ride off to find the sunset together, but this person that intersected my life for this moment of time was quite impactful on my health. Why? Because I was open to a new experience and I brought those important characteristics to this community-level relationship, just as she did for me. We helped each other and both felt part of a larger whole in coming together.

Sometimes, these universe-bringing moments turn community relationships into the unicorn people. When I first began my professional role as a nurse, I met a wonderful person that I served on a community coalition with. As my professional role evolved, I changed employers, and that just happened to be at the same place of employment as this person. Our friendship grew based on that foundation of work we had already shared. She actually ended up becoming my supervisor, mentor, and great friend. She taught me so much about how to be a professional and how to be a better version of myself. You just never know when one of the community relationship folks will turn into a unicorn for you. Be open to what the universe brings you, my friends; there are gifts waiting around every corner!

The last of the Russian nesting dolls is your community as a whole. Not those folks that you come into contact with on a semi-regular basis like we just talked about, but more of the community flavor of the environment you live in. These environmental-level relationships include people that influence the health of your community, like those that serve on your school board, the city council, ward representatives, county boards, local government, the faith community, and even the social norms that influence how your community bridges itself together to make social cohesion stronger, more vibrant, and healthy.

In the community I live in, we host free concerts at a local park down by the river once a week throughout the summer. These concerts host some musicians that travel nationally, so they are pretty darn fun to listen to! There are local food trucks from some amazing restaurateurs, which means great food is always in good supply. The concerts begin at about the time people are getting done with work and wrap up by early evening, so there's no rowdiness or stupidity happening, just good, wholesome family fun.

It is an opportunity to grab a picnic basket, throw down a blanket, eat good food, socialize with friends and neighbors, meet new people, rest and relax, hear some groovy music, and support local businesses. This is just one example of what a healthy community environment that supports social connectedness can look like.

Think to yourself about how the community as a whole that you live in interacts among groups and organizations.

- Do folks support community initiatives and coalitions to better the overall health of the community?
- Do organizations come together to address inequities and help those that are in need?
- Does your community support the arts, green space, inclusivity, local businesses, and peaceful discord?
- Think to yourself, does your community reflect your values?

By choosing to live in a community environment that aligns with your values, you can strengthen relationship bonds in general. Acting as a steward of these values can propel your community as a whole to a healthier state, meaning you and the relationships you have built can act as a change agent for your own health, the health of others, and the health of your community.

Now I also want to note that I use the word "choice" in my definition of a healthy community and where people end up living in terms of lifestyle choices. I have a love-hate relationship with this word choice as it relates to health, because I appreciate that many do not have a choice in their current environment or in certain lifestyle behaviors; more on that in the next chapter, too. For those that do not have that choice in their living environment right now, please consider strengthening the other types of relationships discussed in this chapter to support your health and well-being. This book is not a prescription on what you need to do to change your life, these are simply golden nuggets of information that I am presenting you with, and it is up to you to choose what you act upon, when and if you are able to. We can't change everything all at once, but we can set realistic goals for ourselves if we feel the positive impact has the potential for outweighing any risks that may come with the change.

After reading through the supporting actors information, I have another exercise for you. Stop and think, then jot some notes down to answer these questions:

- Who are my unicorns, and do I make an effort to continue my relationships with them?
- Who/what relationships might be hurting my health?
- Who/what relationships might I be hurting?
- Is there any way I can help to change the dynamic of those that might be hurting my health or for those that I might be harming?
- Are all of my nesting dolls intact, and if not, which doll might need a bit of craftsmanship or a hot glue gun?
- What is the level of strength and beauty of each of my nesting dolls?
- How might I be able to strengthen and beautify my relationships with my unicorns?
- How might I be able to strengthen and beautify my relationships with my community people?
- How might I be able to strengthen and beautify my relationship to my community as a whole?

No judgment here; these are just some questions to get you thinking about what types of relationships you have and how they might be impacting your overall health. Who will make the cut after all the auditions have been completed? Do you need to hold more auditions after your assessment? Do you need to take some acting lessons yourself to make the cut for those that you support and care for?

Earlier in this chapter, I shared an example of a relationship that did not demonstrate healthy characteristics, and I sort of left it at that, simply telling you what about that relationship was unhealthy, how it did not go so well, and how I was negatively affected, but I didn't really breathe life into the specific actions that should be taken if you find yourself in an unhealthy relationship. That is with intent. Only you can determine what is healthy or unhealthy, what supports you and what doesn't, the extent the relationship is impacting your life, and what you have the capacity to change. Most often, this is not a cut-and-dried, black-and-white kind of issue; there are many shades of gray that need to be considered. We may not be able to just get up and walk away from an unhealthy relationship whenever we want to. Sometimes our brother-in-law is always going to be a jerk and there is nothing we can do about it, so we just have to bear down and deal with him as best we can at Thanksgiving dinner. He will more than likely be in your life as long as he continues to be in your sister's or brother's life. Sometimes we have a boss that is simply mean, and we can't just up and quit our job because people depend on us to bring home the bacon. There is no easy answer here, despite everyone else's best-intentioned advice they try to offer you. Yes, the reality is there are unhealthy relationships out there, and sometimes the best and only option for saving your health is to excise them from your life. But more often than not, you will have to learn how to manage unhealthy relationships within your life so as to have the least amount of negative health consequences from them as possible. In the next chapter, we will talk about how to support each of your dimensions of wellness to be the healthiest version of yourself that you can be. Try to embrace some of those interventions to serve as a protective barrier, a sort of second skin, from the negative effects of unhealthy relationships that we might not be able to remove from our lives just yet.

Before we close out this chapter, I wanted to mention that the research is getting clearer about social media versus in-person interactions, since I used this as an example in our unicorn conversation. Relationships and social connectedness via physical interactions fare better at staving off the negative effects of social isolation as opposed to social media or digital interactions. For different reasons over the years, we have systematically replaced many of our personal interactions with digital ones, and it just doesn't cut the mustard. And before anyone starts wagging their finger and blaming "those kids" for not knowing how to socially interact anymore because they are always on their phones, I need you to stop right there and take a long, hard look at yourself. This is not just about kids. Look around. This is not a generational problem, but a societal problem. Why is it that we can't get into an elevator without taking our phones out of our pocket or sit next to a fellow parent on the bleachers without checking our email? When was the last time you went to a restaurant and just sat and visited without your phone on the table or in your hand? Or the last time you stood in a line without scrolling through your social media feed? Now, I am not saying you need to strike up a conversation with anyone and everyone you sit next to wherever you go, or that you can never look at your phone when you have some spare minutes, but perhaps just making eye contact with those around you, smiling, nodding, and acknowledging others' existence can help us reattach to humanity and stoke some healthy social connectedness.

While I have offered you examples of staying connected with friends and family through social media and shared with you how great it is, I want to mention that if your social media interactions are replacing your physical interactions, you might want to reassess your choice. Now I know that we have lived through a revolutionary time in history, when how we interact with humans has completely morphed in a very short amount of time, and we have also lived through a pandemic where our answer to everything was "move it to the digital space." I appreciate that. However, meeting with people face to face is the superior option in terms of your health. Here is the asterisk: if there are true barriers to meeting in person, then it is still better to stay connected through social media and digital spaces than to not stay connected at all. Bottom line: use social media as a stop-gap measure for when you have barriers to meeting in person and to get you through the spells of time when you cannot see each other, but if there are no barriers, schedule a date to meet for a face-to-face visit.

I hope I did not bore you to tears with my nesting doll analogy to help you conceptualize an ecological model of health. This is just one way we can help to explain how various influences and relationships can impact the status of an individual's and a community's health.

The show must go on!

Now, without further ado, on to Act One, where we talk about what health and wellness really mean!

CHAPTER FIVE

ACT ONE

Finally, the moment you have been waiting long enough for! Now you might be thinking, "This is what I bought the book for, get your act together and tell me how to get healthy already!" OK, here's the deal. You're going to tell me first. Now, you're like, "What did you just say?!?!" For real. Take a few minutes to write down what health and wellness means to you. Define it. In three to five sentences, tell me exactly what health and wellness is. And yes, I will be upfront, this is a trick question; this is one of those plot twists. By the end of the next chapter, I will ask you to write down your definition of health and wellness once more and reflect on the changes you made to it. It probably will be different (hopefully!), but go ahead, give it a whirl! We have to start somewhere.

My personal definition of health and wellness:

_____

_____

_____

_____

_____

As we chatted about earlier, if you ask people what it means to be healthy and/or well, most often they will respond with "eating right and working out." While those are two very important considerations to health and well-being, they are by far not the only considerations; health and wellness is much more nuanced than that. In this chapter we will talk about what it really means to be "healthy and well." We will discuss the interplay between the different determinants of health in this chapter, and in the next chapter we will discuss the different dimensions of wellness, and how they all pull and tug on one another to impact your holistic health and wellness. After we cover all of that information, I will share with you my definition of health and wellness, and you will tell me what it means to be healthy and well in your own life in a much more comprehensive manner than what you just wrote (if I do my job right).

There are quite a few different wellness models out there, some with five, six, seven dimensions; you get the idea. In the following chapter, we will discuss eight different dimensions of wellness. As we go through each of them, you will notice some overlap. With poor health in one dimension, you more than likely will have poorer health in another. That is the interdependent nature of health and wellness. Conversely, you will notice that when one dimension is strong it will more than likely tug or pull on at least one other dimension for greater benefit in a sort of ripple effect. I will offer examples of this along our journey together. One more time, remember that this book is not a prescription. You may only be able to make a little change here and there that is sustainable (sustainability is key, and we will talk about how to best achieve that in the next chapter). Honestly, the most impactful health behavior changes to start with are changes in your own perspective toward you, your life, and your situation (recall that "head stuff," like reining in the inner antagonist and embracing Pollyanna, which we talked about earlier).

In terms of interventions for each of the dimensions, start small. Doing too much too quickly can result in what you perceive as "failures" and support a defeatist attitude toward future behavior change. With a positive perspective, when you do embark upon sustainable behavior change, you will more than likely start to see other dimensions improving even without having that original intention. Think back to my panic attack days. I began to work on the panic attacks but in reality, that affected many other dimensions in a domino effect for me as "added perks" along my journey.

But for our work together in this chapter, we will take a closer look at these things called "determinants of health" that are impactful. These three determinants are genetic, social, and environmental. You will need to be aware of these as a sort of baseline measure of where you are in terms of health. They will even help to explain why your current level of health is what it is, right here, right now. Some of these we can change, some we can't, but knowledge is power, my friends, and at the very least you can seek to avoid certain situations, if at all possible, to help maintain or support your health. It is also important to remember shifts in positive perspective and embracing all of the different items we discussed so far in the book when reviewing these determinants. Yes, we may have been handed a subpar deck of cards, but shifting the thought process surrounding those to one of a growth mindset instead of a Negative Nellie mindset can be powerful.

Genetic determinants are pretty much what they sound like: the genetic material that your biological parents handed down to you via the procreation process. We cannot change our genetics (OK, in certain rare instances it can change, but I am not going to go into Spider-Man radiation detail here). I can't change my hair color unless I grab a box of L'Oreal Paris; my hair color is what it is based on my genetic code. I can't change my eye color unless

I want to buy some tinted contacts. That's just my DNA. You get the idea. Some of you may not be aware of your genetic makeup. If you're interested, you may want to consider some genetic testing at some point to get a clearer picture. With the availability and ease of genetic testing at a relatively inexpensive price in the peace of your own home, you can get detailed information if you are so inclined. There are some big feelings surrounding these companies in terms of privacy, Big Brother, and future implications of meta data usage, however, if you are curious and OK with the risk versus reward, it may be beneficial to go down this path in terms of lifestyle changes. As more people participate, the aggregate data get more robust and predictions get stronger, so it may be a useful tool for you to have in your box of props for the next act.

While there are things we just can't change, like our actual genetic makeup, sometimes we can turn on or turn off these genes by changing the expressions of our genes. This is called epigenetics. Epigenetics is a quickly growing scientific field of discovery that everyone should be keeping an eye on. This field has an immense potential to impact health, wellness, diet, environment, illness management, health care delivery, you name it. The subject can be complex and difficult to wrap the brain cells around, so I will offer a very high-level overview of this. If you are interested in a more "heady" read, please review the additional reading information at the end of the book for further details.

Epigenetics can be loosely translated to "changes above the gene." Just to be very clear, epigenetics is not about changing your actual DNA; it simply changes how your body "interprets" or "reads" and expresses your DNA code. In terms of epigenetics, I may experience things that can sort of "flip a switch," for lack of a better analogy, to either activate or deactivate a certain part of my genetic code. And here is the creepy part—it is not just my choices, environment, and lived experiences that can impact my epigenetics; it can be the experiences, environment, and choices that my parents or grandparents made or lived through. The consequences of these lived experiences are cascading and can last through up to four generations (according to the latest research results). Let me share some examples to better understand this concept.

I completed a "23andMe" profile and came to the realization that I am genetically predisposed to acquiring diabetes. This is something I am not interested in developing, so I make daily choices in my eating patterns and diet to avoid developing the disease. So just because I am predisposed to something does not mean that it is a sentence that will 100% be carried out for me. There are choices I can make that help to prevent it from manifesting—basically I am doing everything in my power to not "flip that switch." Some women know that they carry the BRCA gene and make the conscious decision to have a voluntary mastectomy to reduce their chances of acquiring breast cancer. That is a preemptive strike against a genetic predisposition to, again, prevent the flipping of that switch. Think back on what your parents and grandparents may have been blessed or cursed with. Long life? Dementia? Cardiovascular disease? Flexibility, where they can actually touch their toes? You may also be predisposed to these traits and many more, and those predispositions may be turned on or turned off depending on environment, lived experiences, and lifestyle choices. Here are some more epigenetic examples to get you thinking.

Emerging research suggests that older fathers are more likely to have children with autism spectrum disorder. Age, coupled with environmental factors, may trigger epigenetic changes to increase the likelihood of this disorder in their offspring. Other factors change sperm as well; things like marijuana and nicotine use, past traumas, and even diet. These factors can turn on or off those genetic expressions to increase the likelihood of disorders and disease in their offspring. What a woman eats or experiences in pregnancy can be transmitted through epigenetic changes to the infant that can follow the infant through his, her, or their lifespan. As an example, in the 1940s there was a famine in the Netherlands. Following that, children from mothers that were pregnant during that time had a higher likelihood of coronary heart disease and obesity. Identical twins that were raised together with similar upbringings often will have a relatively similar health status; however, twins that have been separated can diverge significantly based on the differences in environment, experiences, and lifestyle. A person can develop cancer triggered by exposure to chemicals in the environment, along with predisposition toward cancer. A trauma a parent or grandparent experienced may result in mental illness in future generations. Living through a trauma like a mass shooting or assault yourself can impact not only your mental and physical health, but that of your descendants as well.

As we go through all of the dimensions of wellness in the next chapter, I hope that you reflect on what you and your parents or grandparents may have experienced and ask yourself if these experiences may be impacting your past, current, or future wellbeing either positively or negatively. This is not doom and gloom; just because you or your past lineage had some not-so-great habits or lived experiences, you can still embrace that shifting of life perspective we talked about earlier, and perhaps work on some small behavior changes that might propel you toward a healthier state and prevent epigenetic switches from flipping. Honestly, only about 10% of health outcomes are linked to genetics. And some more good news—epigenetic changes are not necessarily permanent. Changes can take place in response to your environment and lifestyle changes, which means that moving more, eating less, living in a non-polluted environment, sleeping better, not smoking, volunteering, and many other health behaviors we will discuss shortly all contribute to diminishing the increased risks of epigenetic changes that might hurt your health.

Before we move on, I would like you to jot down some thoughts you have on how your genetics or epigenetics might be helping or hurting your current health state.

Helping:

Hurting:

Next up are the social determinants of health (SDOH), and these are the most impactful, so pull up a chair while we have this chat. While genetics account for a minimal portion of our health outcomes (which is great, because there is not too much we can do to change our DNA unless we want a freaky spider bite), SDOH accounts for the majority of impact. Approximately 40% of our health outcomes are influenced by SDOH.

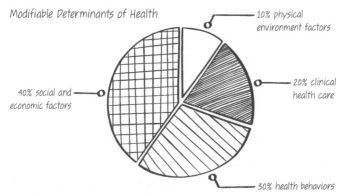

Source: Park, H., Roubal, A. M., Jovaag, A., Gennuso, K. P., & Catlin, B. B. (2015). Relative contributions of a set of health factors to selected health outcomes. *American Journal of Preventive Medicine* 49(6), 961–69. doi: 10.1016/j.amepre.2015.07.016.

Health care systems are required to spend a certain percentage of their profits on community benefits, which often are directed toward SDOH concerns. Public health systems, from the Centers for Disease Control all the way down to your local public health offices, direct a fair share of their resources to address SDOH. Kaiser Permanente invests about $3 billion to address SDOH. Why is that? Because they are so very impactful to the current health and health outcomes of individuals, groups, communities, and societies. Focusing on SDOH is where we can get the most bang for our buck in terms of impacting health. Unfortunately, changes to these areas are slow, can be painstaking to effect change in, and are difficult to measure. These interventions are not flashy new treatments or medications; most often they are primary prevention activities, things you do to prevent diseases before they start, and primary prevention activities most often do not deliver on the "wow" factor like a new treatment, medication, or surgery does. The social determinants of health reflect the values of the communities we live in, meaning our health can depend on where our communities are investing their resources—more on zip codes in a bit.

You see, SDOH basically boils down to three little words: "access to resources." What kind of resources, you ask? Throw a dart; you will hit one. Included in the next graphic, you will see an overview of resources from the Kaiser Family Foundation. Go through this listing to get a better understanding of them and to determine which resources you have access to or do not have access to. The more you have access to economic stability, a safe neighborhood and environment, quality education, healthy and affordable foods, community connectedness, and health care, the more likely it is you will be a healthier person and live longer.

Social Determinants of Health

Economic Stability	Neighborhood and Physical Environment	Education	Food	Community and Social Context	Health Care System
Employment	Housing	Literacy	Hunger	Social integration	Health coverage
Income	Transportation	Language	Access to healthy options	Support systems	Provider availability
Expenses	Safety	Early childhood education		Community engagement	Provider linguistic and cultural competency
Debt	Parks				
Medical bills	Playgrounds	Vocational training		Discrimination	
Support	Walkability	Higher education		Stress	Quality of care
	Zip code/ geography				

Health Outcomes
Mortality, Morbidity, Life Expectancy, Health Care Expenditures, Health Status, Functional Limitations

After going through this list, write down what resources you have secure access to:

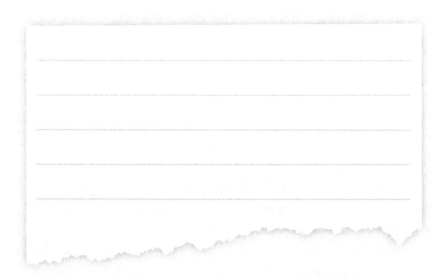

Some of you might be thinking "duh," of course you are going to be healthier if you have access to health care, Carrie. Well, you are right—that is a part of SDOH, but a very small part. Health care (for the most part) is there for when you are already sick and need help. The bulk of health care dollars are used to heal illness, injury, and disease, or at least to try to stop the progression of what is ailing you. Access to resources such as a living-wage job, healthy and affordable food, quality education, social cohesion, and a safe neighborhood are things we can address to help stop diseases, illnesses, and injuries before they even start, aka primary prevention. Remember that old adage grandma used to tell you? "An ounce of prevention is worth a pound of cure?" Well, grandma was wise with that one. It is far more cost effective to prevent XYZ disease with upstream interventions than it is to control its cascading effects, like lost work time, family caregiver time and effort, and emotional distress. This basically means that if the list of resources you wrote down that you had access to was lengthy, you will have better health and health outcomes. If your list was short, you are at risk for poorer health and health outcomes.

Let me use some examples to better clarify this topic, starting with me, since you already know a bit of my background. I was born in a white, middle-class family with two parents, I experienced no ACEs, and I lived in a rural, non-polluted environment. I have not experienced racial prejudice. I had access to green spaces to climb trees, jump in puddles, and ride my bike. My neighborhood was uber safe. I had access to a quality private education, kindergarten through senior year of high school, and because of that solid foundation, I was able to attend and be successful in many years of postsecondary education after that. I was able to secure living-wage jobs based off of that postsecondary education I obtained. We always had enough food on the table, some of which came from our own garden that was free of pesticides. Our friends, family, and neighbors were tightly connected, and I have always had continuous medical coverage. A large part of why I am in a state of health and well-being is because of these items I just listed. Let's take a look at a case study to better understand the flip side of this.

A Latina girl born into a single-parent household with loose social connectedness to friends, family, or neighbors means the child and parent may not have the support needed for their emotional health, and their overall health may be strained related to limited physical and financial support as well. Being a child of color increases the likelihood of experiencing chronic racism. Living in a single-parent household increases the risk of being economically disadvantaged, and being a female of racial minority coupled with being economically disadvantaged also places the child at higher risk for experiencing ACEs during childhood. Those that are economically disadvantaged will more than likely live in a community that is less safe, has fewer green spaces, and has poorer access to quality education, as schools in under-resourced areas typically have a smaller tax base to fund them. Fewer green spaces mean fewer opportunities to connect with nature and neighbors. Higher crime, hence less safe neighborhoods, results in chronic stress responses and less daily physical movement. If a parent is afraid of violence in the neighborhood, the child will more than likely spend more time indoors to protect their safety, which means less physical activity and a higher chance of obesity and its associated illnesses. Many economically disadvantaged neighborhoods are food deserts and food swamps, which diminishes access to fresh and affordable foods and increases risk for chronic diseases like metabolic disorders (such as diabetes). Low-performing schools most often do not attract exceptional teachers, since there are—you guessed it—less resources to help support their work in the classroom, poorer wages than more affluent neighboring schools, and they may be subject to collective shaming for the low standardized test scores of the population they serve. Low-performing schools typically have larger classroom sizes due to budgetary constraints, which can lead to poor social cohesion, lower standardized test scores, and higher dropout rates. This in turn will limit opportunities to attend and be successful in quality postsecondary schools, which results in poor access to living-wage jobs. Poor access to living-wage jobs can mean stitching together two or three part-time jobs to make ends meet, which means no access to health care benefits or a regular schedule. Without a regular schedule, sleep patterns are disturbed, and even if access to health care is a possibility through public insurance, it may not be an option to get time off of work (without repercussions) to actually use those health care benefits.

This case study helps to demonstrate a poor "access to resources" cycle and how that poor access can greatly diminish one's health in many areas. Now, this is just a tiny slice of what the social determinants are. I could literally teach a semester-long class just on this topic, but I wanted to share this example with you so that you can appreciate the interconnectedness of health (or lack thereof) when it comes to SDOH. It is often a slippery slope; you can't affect one without a domino effect. Where you live, work, play, and pray are all impacted either positively or negatively by SDOH.

You may recall my bugaboo with that "lifestyle choices" terminology I brought up earlier. So much of this work surrounding SDOH stems from the circumstances that you were born into. Yes, we all have free will. Yes, we have all grown up with the concept of the American Dream and the "pull yourself up by your bootstraps" pep talk that is freely given to most everyone in America, but it can be extraordinarily difficult to pull oneself out of many of these circumstances. Asking a question like "So why don't you just move if your neighborhood is so bad?" to a person stuck in this cycle doesn't really work. When you are living paycheck to paycheck, how can you save money for moving expenses and first and last month's rent, find a new job in a new community where you may or may not be accepted, or be discriminated against with a lack of any social or familial support? Asking "Why don't you just study harder and then you can get better grades and get into college?" might not work either. If the person has experienced ACEs or has not had access to early childhood education, their reading and comprehension skills and social, emotional, and mental health capacity may be diminished. What about "Why don't you just lose the weight; you wouldn't have such high blood sugar then?" That sounds great on paper too, but when you only have access to the two-pound bag of shelf-stable pretzels and costly overripe vegetables at the local bodega, the pretzels usually win out. This is not about pulling oneself up by the bootstraps, but rather making life equitable to support the health of everyone, not just a few that were born into a cushy spot in this world. In other words, supporting health equity. Health equity means that everyone has the opportunity to reach their full potential. This is different from equality. Equality means you give everyone the same thing in order to be on a level playing field. Equity means you put everyone on the same playing field, along with unique adaptive equipment addressing their differences. Here is a good graphic of what equity looks like in action, as opposed to an equality premise.

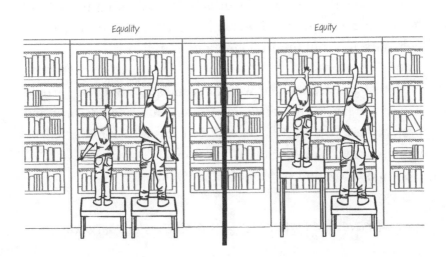

Think all of this talk about "choices" and all of this health equity stuff is just a bad trailer to a B movie? Let's consult the data. A very simple tool to depict the linkage between SDOH and health outcomes is your zip code. Yup, you heard me right, your zip code. Tell me where you live, and I will tell you what your life expectancy is. Life expectancy can differ as much as 20 years from zip code to zip code, neighborhood to neighborhood. I will give you three guesses on what impacts the life expectancies from neighborhood to neighborhood, and the first two don't count: yup, social determinants—access to resources.

> To determine what your life expectancy is based on your zip code, scan the QR code with your phone or type rwjf.ws/3PjUhmo into your browser.

For the first time in history, our children are expected to live shorter lives than we will. With SODH accounting for 40% of health outcomes, we need to stand up and take notice to not only help ourselves, but future generations as well.

Now that you are familiar with the concept of SDOH, I would like you to pause and reflect on where you live, work, play, and pray, and ask yourself what kind of access you have to the following resources. A ranking of "1" is crickets at curtain call, and "4" is a standing ovation at the end of Act One.

I have adequate access to a safe neighborhood.

1   2   3   4

I have adequate access to safe and affordable housing.

1   2   3   4

I have adequate access to a living-wage job.

1   2   3   4

I have adequate access to a quality education.

1   2   3   4

I have access to daily life activities without prejudice.

1   2   3   4

I have adequate access to healthy and affordable foods.

1   2   3   4

I have adequate access to social connectedness.

1   2   3   4

I have adequate access to health care.

1   2   3   4

SDOH really impact health quite a bit, and you all know by now I am stickler about this "choices" word, since so many of these things have been dealt to us and not chosen. Yes, we all have free will and can make our own choices, but some of these choices are made for us without us even thinking about or realizing it. So what can you, I, we do about this issue? Well, first things first: we need to look at our perspective. Simply switching on that gratitude practice and growth mindset can help. Second, make little changes where you can, like working out at home if your neighborhood is not safe, or growing produce in container gardens on your patio if you live in a food desert or food swamp. Or taking free online courses to build your skill sets to help climb the employment ladder. Meeting your neighbors and making that connection to build social cohesion. Starting a neighborhood watch. Volunteering at the local school. Attending local zoning committee meetings to voice your opinion on the need for walkable, safe neighborhoods. Voting. Yes, the barriers are real and sometimes can feel overwhelming. Trying one small thing to support your health and the health of your community in this realm can help you build your confidence and make you feel more in control of your life and your health outcomes.

Now it is your turn! What is one thing you could do right now to support your SDOH? Or if yours are pretty secure, what about your neighborhood or your community? How might you strengthen SDOH looking at this topic through that lens? Go ahead and jot down your notes here:

The last of the determinants that we will chat about are environmental determinants of health. Just like an actor needs a stage that is clean and safe to sing and dance, you too need an environment that limits pollutants and chemicals to live a healthy life. Our natural and built environment, such as the buildings we live in and nature that surrounds us, impacts health outcomes. Things that can harm us in this realm are exposure to chemicals through air, land, and water pollution, and environmental changes related to climate change.

Chemicals are everywhere: in your hand soap, plastic bottles, home cleaning products, car exhaust, you name it; they are all over the place. Most often your body can handle the exposures without ill effect, but depending on your genetics, the state of your immune system, other diseases or illnesses you may already have, and the amount of exposure, they can cause health problems. We know that exposure to lead in drinking water can cause learning disabilities, mercury in our food can cause birth defects, asbestos can cause respiratory disorders and cancer, and nitrates from fertilizers in our food and water systems can cause impaired oxygen exchange and cardiovascular problems. Chemicals in the air, land, water, and built environment can be harmful to us in many different ways. These are just a few that have research to demonstrate causation, but think of how many other chemicals there are in our daily environment that we have yet to discover the linkages between exposure and ill health effects.

Throwaway plastics, from water bottles to dollar store beach toys, are easy targets when we think of ways to decrease our pollution footprint, but think about other items you might be able to act a bit more conservatively with. Do you know the true costs of that pair of jeans hanging in your closet? How many pairs do you have? Each of those pairs uses thousands of gallons of water to make and that water, polluted with chemicals and heavy metals, gets dumped into waterways—so much so that the bulk of Asia's rivers and lakes are polluted. The textile industry alone has a daunting environmental footprint. These factories increase carbon dioxide levels in the air, plus contribute to land and water pollution and to an ever-growing landfill problem. Think about all of the jeans you have owned in your lifetime. Most of them are in a landfill somewhere. According to the EPA, in 1960 the United States produced about 1,760 thousand tons of textiles and landfilled the bulk of that. In 2018, the latest data shared by the EPA, Americans generated 17,030 thousand tons, with about 11,000 of those being landfilled. Americans throw away 70 pounds of clothing per year, per person (EPA, 2022). How many articles of clothing do you own? How many do you need to own? This is just the textile industry. This problem is obviously not just clothing. Stop and think about everything sitting in your garbage can right now. Processed food wrappers, old food, plastic shopping bags, batteries, takeout containers. That all goes somewhere. How much do you contribute to landfills?

I'd like to demonstrate the impact of chemical pollution, community call to action, and individual choice by, you guessed it, sharing a story with you. Back in 1996, Atlanta, Georgia, hosted the Olympic Games. The city was expecting a large influx of people between athletes, their entourages, and spectators. Because of this, the Atlanta city government asked their citizens to refrain from private auto use as much as possible. In addition to this call to action, they asked for people to embrace carpooling, worked with local employers to offer employees more flexible and remote work schedules, and added additional bus and train routes to encourage public transit usage. This call to action worked! Even with the addition of one million visitors to the city, air pollution from car exhaust fell, ozone pollution was reduced by about 28%, and, as a positive health repercussion of this, so did asthma emergencies. That's right, by reducing car exhaust, children who had asthma and were receiving medical assistance (those that are most vulnerable to this disease) had about a 40% reduction in emergency room visit rates during this time. Individuals chose to drive less or to carpool. Communities came together to promote mass transit. Employers supported employees. We saw positive health results. Magic happened! From individual choices came a collective of choices that significantly impacted the health of the community. That is pretty darn amazing. This is just one small example of how individuals can come together to impact environmental health and well-being. There are a ton of examples out there. If the problems seem too big, keep these examples in mind. Every little bit helps. From choosing not to buy that ninth pair of jeans to walking to work instead of driving, it all makes a difference.

Climate change impacts our environmental determinants of health as well. With climate change we will continue to see increasing droughts, floods, heat waves, hurricane frequency and intensity, wildfires, rising sea levels, insect outbreaks, tree disease, algal blooms, greater ocean acidity, and more. Conversely, there will be decreasing potable water supplies, agricultural yields, and decreasing choices to avert the growing crises. Here is the thing about environmental determinants as they relate to climate change: they are linked with SDOH for a double whammy. Those with the least access to resources are at the greatest risk from the effects of climate change, and I am not just talking about third-world countries, but folks everywhere, including the United States. Let me share another example.

With climate change comes higher heat. This is most pronounced in urban areas. Those that live in cities can be trapped in what's called a heat island. Heat islands occur because buildings, roads, and manmade structures absorb heat more than trees and bodies of water do. Urban areas that have few green spaces (remember those social determinants we just talked about?) become these islands of high heat. High heat can cause heat exhaustion, exacerbation of other illnesses such as asthma and cardiovascular disease, and death. In the 2003 European heat wave, more than 70,000 people in Europe died. Each year, with increasing frequency, folks in the United States die from high heat. Young children and older adults, those with chronic conditions, the economically disadvantaged, and folks working outdoors for a living are at increased risk for poorer health outcomes with increased temperatures. Crime rates even increase as the temperature rises. Electricity demands soar with increased air conditioning use, which in turn increases the risks of blackouts and less reprieve from the heat when those air conditioners no longer have the electricity needed to run them. When you couple the rising temperatures of climate change with heat islands in areas that are under-resourced, you have a recipe for a health disaster. This is just one small example of how climate change can impact our health. There are countless other examples I could have used; maybe that will be the next book. . . .

Ever hear the term "not in my backyard"? It basically means that those who are more affluent and more well-resourced have a stronger collective voice in preventing or dismantling systems that hurt the health or attractiveness of their community. (Is this reminiscent of SDOH?) A new landfill has to be created because the old one is at capacity? A chemical plant is moving into town? Wastewater needs to be dumped somewhere? A new concentrated animal feeding operation (CAFO), aka factory farm, needs a place to be built? Where do you think that will go? Into the neighborhood that is too economically challenged and with poorer resources to object to this. Under-resourced neighborhoods typically have looser social connectedness and cohesion to come together to protest in unity. They have fewer financial resources to hire lawyers for lengthy court battles, and they typically do not have the human capital to lobby local, state, and federal officials for change. So these neighborhoods and people living there that are already impacted negatively by SDOH get more sick, bearing the burden of chronic disease related to their environmental determinants.

What can you do? I know you are probably tired of hearing this, but reduce, reuse, and recycle. I'm not sure about you, but I just get so overwhelmed when shopping sometimes. Everything I look at when I go into a store forces me to think about where it will all end up. Eventually we know where it will all go, right? In a landfill, slowly leaching chemicals into the soil and water and taking thousands of years to decompose. UGH. What to do? The first step is to reduce. Think to yourself before you buy that new shirt or that package of disposable forks, do you really need it? Is it really that painful to take real forks on your picnic? Can you find a "new" shirt at a consignment or resale shop? Next, reuse. I have to say that while I am not the biggest fan out there for metadata collection from social media, the Facebook Marketplace has become my friend. When I have something I don't use anymore, I literally just post that on the Marketplace with the label "free to a good home," and nine times out of ten it works within hours! My old cooler, hot plate, or spring coat is gone in minutes, reused by someone who is excited to have it and can breathe a bit more life into it. Finally, recycle. If you have to buy something, figure out first if its packaging or the item itself is recyclable, and choose that option over those that are not recyclable. Instead of using plastic food storage containers I use Mason jars. I get way more life out of those, no chemicals leach into my foods, and when they get old, worn, and chipped, the glass is recyclable.

Does this problem feel too big? The environmental determinants are about the built environment and larger policies and systems that are shaped by government, politics, and wealth, but you can use your purchasing power to make some changes here. If you refrain from purchasing chemicals, throw away plastics, and avoid overconsuming in general, you are using that purchasing power to reduce industrial pollution. Need some more ideas to get you started on how you can support your environmental determinants of health in ways that don't feel too overwhelming? Here are a few of my favorites. Instead of using plastic shopping bags, I always take cloth bags or a backpack when I shop. Instead of buying processed foods at the supermarket, I walk to the farmer's market with those cloth bags and buy meat and produce from local farmers, and those items don't have any cellophane surrounding them. Plant a tree. Use bar soap instead of liquid soap. Use your front yard as a pollinator garden instead of boring old grass (less mowing, too!). Use a rain barrel to water your plants. Buy local. Don't buy throwaway plastics. Walk more, drive less. Use public transit. Support the creation of green spaces in your community. Create a community garden. Choose to buy from companies that are eco-friendly. Vote. Little changes. Baby steps. Easy peasy.

Your turn! What can you do to keep your stage nice and tidy and support your overall health and well-being?

Jot down some ways you might be able to limit chemical exposures through your food, water, air, or built environment.

Jot down some ideas here on some small changes you might be willing to embrace to reduce, reuse, and/or recycle.

Overall, how do you think you can use the information about the genetic, social, and environmental determinants of health to support your own health and well-being? What about that of your neighbors and your community? Does the information you learned about the determinants of health align with your personal definition that you created at the beginning of this chapter? Jot down those ideas here:

___

The show must go on!

Now that we have reviewed the determinants of health, we will move into the next chapter, where we will take a closer look at each of the dimensions of wellness. Working in the different dimensions of wellness can be a bit less daunting or overwhelming, because we have a bit more control over those when compared to the determinants of health.

CHAPTER SIX

THE DRAMATIC ARC

Now onto the dimensions of wellness! While the determinants impact your life and health outcomes, they can be outside of your locus of control in some ways. The dimensions of wellness are those areas personal to you that you have the most behavioral change capacity. As I mentioned earlier, we will be discussing eight different dimensions, what they are, and what they "look like" in action, along with some ideas on how to support each of the dimensions. Watch for those ripple effects throughout, too!

Let's just jump right into this, shall we? The first dimension we will discuss is the financial dimension. Let's just get money out of the way right off the bat. Can money make you happier? Healthier? Well, sometimes. It can afford you safety and security to meet your basic needs, but just like anything else in this world, sometimes too much of a good thing can be a bad thing. On one side of the coin, if you do not earn enough money to meet your basic needs like food and housing, then you more than likely are not financially well. On the flip side of that coin, if you have so much money that you spend wastefully and constantly crave more despite the consequences of excess, then that is not so healthy or well either. There are two parts to financial wellness. The first is having enough financial stability to meet your needs and the second is to attain satisfaction with the amount of financial stability you have. The key is finding the balance between the two that is right for you and your situation.

First things first: we need to have a quick little chat about Maslow's hierarchy of needs. Yes, I know this is not a textbook, but as you can see there are some data, research, and behavioral change theories integrated into any wellness conversation to better appreciate its impact, so hopefully you are finding the information interesting at the very least. Maslow's hierarchy is this psychological model that health folks use all the time. And I mean like All. The. Time. It's sort of a home base. In the model there are five levels in the shape of a pyramid. The first two levels comprise our basic needs like food and water and shelter (level one) and safety and security (level two). The following two levels are about meeting our psychological needs, and the tippy top of the pyramid is about realizing our full potential.

Level one includes things like adequate housing, clothing, a heat source in cold weather, food to eat, water to drink, and sex—yup, we all need to procreate to keep the human race going. All those things that sustain basic life. Once a human achieves that first level, then they are able to move on up a step of the pyramid to work on safety and security. These are things like living in a safe neighborhood, community law and order, having access to police and fire services, securing financial stability, and having access to medical care when needed (remind you of the social determinants at all?). After safety and security needs are met, then one can travel up the pyramid to the next level, which addresses our psychological needs. This step in the pyramid is all about relationship building and securing our love and belonging needs—remember Chapter Four? In this area humans work on developing a sense of community through interconnectedness and building intimacy and trust with other humans by being a part of a community. All those unicorns and community relationships are the focus here. The next step in the pyramid is that of esteem. This is where the individual starts to take pride in oneself by way of mastering tasks, being independent, setting goals, and accomplishing achievements in life. This incorporates self-esteem but also securing respect from others. In action, this looks like getting a promotion at work or having your kid tell you that you are a good parent. Finally, the top of the pyramid is the level of self-actualization.

This is where the magic happens! Self-actualization means that you have the ability to be the best version of yourself that you can be! In real life this looks like a person taking risks and being vulnerable to maximize potential and self-growth. An example of self-actualization is achieving a milestone goal. It could be to complete an advanced degree, run a marathon, or strive to be as healthy in each dimension of wellness as possible.

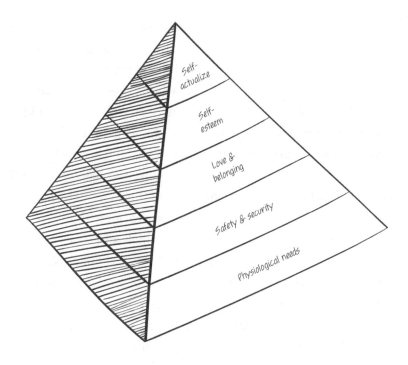

Take a gander at the picture of what this model is so that you can visualize the different levels. Remember that without achieving a lower level, one cannot (or at least it is not very easy to) "move upward" to the next level in a meaningful way. Here is a concrete example to put this into perspective. "I need to have a home before I can live in a safe neighborhood. I have to live in a safe neighborhood before I can develop strong relationships with my neighbors. I have to have strong relationships with my neighbors before I can feel a sense of achievement in organizing a neighborhood coalition to move a community health goal forward, like getting a crossing guard at a busy intersection for the kids walking to school. And then after I accomplish that health goal, perhaps I can achieve self-actualization knowing that all of these moving magical parts came together to help support my health, my family's' health, and my community's health." Bringing it back to the storytelling analogy and everything we have covered so far:

> Physiological needs: I first have to have a stage to be able to be the lead actor in my story (connected with the social determinants of health).
>
> Safety needs: I have to make sure my stage is clean and free of hazards (connected with the environmental determinants of health).
>
> Belongingness and love needs: I have to have good chemistry with my supporting actors and actresses and be confident that they have my back if I forget my lines (connected with relationship building and the social determinants of health).
>
> Esteem needs: I can then be proud of all the hard work we put into the endeavor as evidenced by our fantastic dress rehearsal before we hit opening night on Broadway (connected with quieting our inner critic, relationship building, and supporting our gratitude practice).
>
> Self-actualization needs: And finally, I can have this great sense of accomplishment knowing that I maximized my full potential when I gave it my all and then got a standing ovation at the curtain call of opening night (connected to embracing all of the health and wellness interventions discussed in this book).

So why did I diverge to tell you about this Maslow stuff in the first of the dimensions? Money makes the world go round. And without money you are not able to achieve the first two steps of the pyramid, which means the other stuff is out of reach. As a nurse, I can't have a truly meaningful conversation with a pregnant mom about avoiding risky sexual encounters during the pregnancy if she is homeless and doesn't know where her next meal is coming from. If you live in a neighborhood that is unsafe, it is not too realistic to have a conversation about getting 10,000 steps a day if you are worried about getting mugged (or worse) when you are getting those steps in. We have to meet these basic needs first before we can effect health and wellness changes.

I think everyone is probably aware of the federal poverty guideline, or at least you are familiar with the term(s). The federal poverty level (FPL) is another word for this. These guidelines are used to help identify who qualifies for certain programs such as Medical Assistance, Temporary Assistance for Needy Families (TANF), or Head Start. The threshold is super low. In 2021, the federal poverty level was $12,880 annually for a family of one. I think we can all agree that someone who makes this or less cannot meet their basic needs without help. Think about how much it costs per month for rent, food, and heat; all of those basic needs we just talked about are not being met at or below the FPL.

But there is another term that most people are probably not as familiar with, and that is ALICE. ALICE is an acronym for asset limited, income constrained, and employed. These folks earn more than the FPL, but not enough to make ends meet each month, and many times not enough to qualify for additional resources. So they may be able to pay for rent and heat, but there may not be enough left over for food or unexpected expenses, like a car breaking down or a medical problem. Families have to make tough choices about either paying for rent or paying for prescriptions. Paying for food or paying the heat bill. Want to know who ALICE families are? Those that are taking care of children in daycare, checking out groceries at the store, and caring for grandparents in the nursing home. Hard-working folks that have jobs, but simply do not make enough at those jobs to make ends meet each month. In 2018, 42% of American households couldn't make ends meet.

To see how your state fares in terms of ALICE numbers, scan the QR code with your phone or type bit.ly/3OuQT6V into your browser.

Those at or below the FPL line cannot meet the first level of Maslow's needs. ALICE households will struggle with the second step of the pyramid. This is why we need to talk about the financial dimension of wellness first and why we need to talk about the social determinants of health before we get to the other stuff. Without access to a living-wage job, folks are going to struggle in most other dimensions of wellness because of the interconnected nature of each. Here we go again, Negative Nellie Carrie. Sorry—I need to stop bringing you guys down! OK, this is not all doom and gloom. Here comes Pollyanna. Now more than ever, companies are willing to hire for the person and train for the position. There are free online courses through portals like Coursera that offer classes from prestigious colleges so that you can build employable skill sets. Flipping your perspective to one of gratitude and positivity can open doors. Embracing positivity can help you build relationships, like we talked about in Chapter Four, that can help you to network to find new jobs or build career pathways within your current role (it's not what you know, but who you know!). There are many different interventions to embrace that can help to foster financial security. It can be a slow road and there are many barriers, but it is doable.

The second part o' health in this dimension is that satisfaction piece. I used to think to myself, "If I could just make this amount of money, I would be happy," and then I would make that much and not feel any different. I would set a new goal, accomplish that, same thing. It seems as though us humans have a propensity to spend what we bring in. We make more, we get a bigger house, a new car, go to restaurants more often, buy that new pair of jeans just because, and so on. So, it wasn't necessarily that I was not making enough money, but rather that I wasn't happy with how much I was making. There is a difference there. Everyone's finances are unique to them based on their situation, needs, and values. Once you identify what those needs and values are that drive your finances, and then align those to your financial choices, you can be satisfied with how much you make and live within your means; hence, your health in this dimension strengthens. The key to financial wellness is first securing those basic needs and then developing a sense of satisfaction with what you are making, and living within your budget. If your income goes up from there, great! That is the cherry on top of your sundae. Here are some ways to strengthen your financial wellness once you have met those basic needs, accepted your finances, and are OK with where you are at.

> Create a monthly budget (and stick to it)
>
> Put some money aside each month for any surprise expenditures that come up (like that car breaking down or the medical problem)
>
> Grow your own food (even if it is just a couple tomato plants in containers on the balcony!)

Starting and then contributing to a retirement account on a regular basis

Cook at home instead of going out

If you have the means, desire, and ability, go back to school

Shop at resale stores

Sell things you no longer use at resale stores

Ask yourself before your next purchase, "Is this a need to have or a nice to have?", and then try stick to the need to haves

If it is not a "need to have" but there is still a desire for the item, try to avoid impulse buys by thinking about the purchase for a predetermined amount of time before you click "buy"

Talk to your supervisor and co-workers about any type of career pathway or other employment laddering opportunities in the company or at other companies (it's best to keep the "other company" conversation for the co-workers instead of the supervisor)

Find free community events for entertainment (don't forget about your local library)

Investigate community resources that you might be able to use so as to free up money in other areas of the budget (check with your local United Way or 211 to see what is available)

Try to avoid taking on debt

Try to pay down the debt you have, starting with the debt that has the highest interest rate

Walk instead of drive

Buy produce when it is in season and inexpensive, and then freeze to use it later

Use reusable items instead of consumable items (remember those forks for your picnic)

Now it's your turn! Tell me what your strengths and opportunities are in this dimension. And by opportunities, I mean areas of potential growth, otherwise known as weaknesses—but I don't like that word either, so from here on, out let's agree we will only use the word "opportunity" for areas we can work on.

Strengths:

Opportunities:

Next up, I want you to write down one or two things that you might realistically be able to do in the next couple of months to support your financial dimension of wellness. This could be something as simple as taking your bike to work one day a week or paying down your student loans more aggressively by paying more than the minimum amount due. Just make sure that they are realistic for you to do.

Intervention(s):

_____

_____

_____

_____

Now that we have discussed what humans need in terms of financial wellness, we can move on to the intellectual dimension of wellness. The intellectual dimension outlines the importance of personal growth via our inquisitive minds and also the collective knowledge of our species. Ahh yes, here we return to the backbone of our storytelling enterprise! Humans have passed stories on through the ages as a way to impart our knowledge from generation to generation, so we don't have to start all over again from scratch. Just think if we had to reinvent the wheel or figure out the laws of gravity with every generation, or if we had to relearn that skunks and porcupines don't like to be spooked, or that we need to cook chicken to 165 degrees. We would all be in a pretty tough space, and we definitely would not be as evolved as we currently are. Our knowledge just keeps growing and growing with each passing generation. Knowledge seeking is embedded in our genetic code. Watch babies and toddlers. They explore their environment constantly to gain knowledge. It is this naturally occurring inquisitiveness and curiosity that propels our species. Here is the important part for intellectual health. We need to hold on tight to that natural curiosity throughout the lifespan to continuously support our health in this dimension. Not only do we have to hold on to and harness that curiosity, but we need to revel in it. When a child asks 87 questions in a five-minute time frame, it can get a wee bit overwhelming; however, there is an excitement and joy that comes to a person's soul when asking about, exploring, and learning something new. Call me a teacher at heart, but this process is so beautiful!

Some of you may be thinking, "I did not like school, and I am so very happy that I am done, and I will never ever have to go back." And the teacher in me would respond that that is totally OK, you don't have to, and you can still be healthy and well in this dimension! Weren't expecting that response, were you? Here is the thing with intellectual wellness: the default response for many people on how to support this dimension is "go to school" or "go back to school." While I am not going to dispute this—it is a great way to support this dimension—it is most assuredly not the only way. Think about something you are naturally curious about, like why dogs sniff each other's backsides, or why a 90,000-pound hunk of metal can stay in the air for 12 hours to get you to Paris. Then brainstorm ways on how you can satisfy that curiosity. That is how you support this dimension! You could check out a

Cesar Millan book at the local library to get your sniffing question answered, or you could watch a *National Geographic* special on how airplanes propel themselves upward and forward despite so much gravity trying to pull them downward. Let's say you want to be able to change your own headlight out of your car so that you can save some money (hence supporting your financial dimension of wellness). You could consult a manual and watch YouTube videos to figure this out. That way you are learning a new skill, expanding your knowledge of car ownership, and supporting your intellectual and financial health. It is a little bit like your own research project. You start with a burning question (your natural curiosity) and then you start looking for the answers to quench that curiosity (actions supporting your health).

Many people are worried about dementia, and rightfully so. By 2030, the World Health Organization predicts that about 82 million people will suffer from this disease. Thinking and using our grey matter is just like any other skill. You need to practice keeping it healthy and functioning well. One way (just one—there are many other interventions to embrace, including work in the other dimensions) is to keep using your brain. Using your brain by doing things like crossword and Sudoku puzzles, recalling sports statistics from your childhood, knitting, and learning a foreign language are just some of the ways to support your intellectual wellness and to help prevent dementia from developing.

Let me share a great story about supporting intellectual wellness. My parents are lifelong readers. I remember that my mom always had a book in her hand as she fell asleep when I was a kid, and still does to this day. My dad, who has zero background in health care, stays up in the evenings sitting at the kitchen counter reading old medical textbooks, "just because it's interesting." He writes notes to himself about surgical procedures and diagnostic data. Not that he is ever going to try to remove a gallbladder on someone, it is just because he has a thirst for knowledge, and he is curious about how the human body works. During the pandemic, my parents played cards every day at 4 pm. This helped to keep them sharp, engaged, and intellectually stimulated. Activities like this will support the intellectual dimension and in turn can prevent brain disease in older adulthood.

Finally, be sure to acknowledge your educational experiences and find workarounds for any intellectual dimension challenges. Some of you may feel vulnerable in this dimension based on past lived experiences in a structured school setting. Try to let those past negative experiences go and focus on ways you can support this dimension that are fun for you. For example, I know not everyone enjoys reading. If that is not your thing, get an audio version of the book or watch a documentary. Here are some other ways you might consider supporting your intellectual dimension of health, other than going back to school, that might be fun and exciting.

> Download a language phone app and start learning
>
> Practice the new language with a friend
>
> Go see a local play or musical
>
> Watch documentaries and other nonfiction movies or television series like cooking shows so that you can grill a perfect burger for your friend
>
> "Travel" the world touring historic sites and museums via online event offerings (with Rick Steves!)
>
> Travel the world and immerse yourself in local culture
>
> Go to a museum

Check out a book at the library

Operate your own little lending library so you can swap books with others

Take a "fun" continuing education class at your local technical college

Start or join a book club

Paint by number

Crochet

Learn how to cook a new recipe

Play cribbage, cards, or learn a new board game

Read the news to stay on top of current events; just make sure you are getting that information from a reputable source, like a nonpartisan outlet or a source that is abroad, like the BBC

Now it's your turn! Tell me what your strengths and opportunities are in this dimension.

Strengths:

Opportunities:

_____
_____
_____

Next up, I want you to write down one or two things that you might realistically be able to do in the next couple of months to support your intellectual dimension of wellness. Just make sure that they are realistic for you to do.

Intervention(s):

_____
_____
_____

The occupational dimension closely aligns with both the intellectual and financial dimensions, since often you will go to school to learn a skill, get a job in that field, and secure a paycheck from that job, so it seems like a natural progression to move onward to this dimension next. The occupational dimension, as I mentioned, most often is all about your job. But you may be thinking, what happens if I don't have a job; can I just skip this section? That is a hard "nope." Maybe you are a full-time student, a stay-at-home parent, retired, disabled, independently wealthy . . . you name it. There are many different reasons that one might not have a "for pay" job, but that does not excuse you from reading this section of the book because we all have an occupational dimension that needs some attention, no matter your current role. The occupational dimension is about preparing for and engaging in work that satisfies you, enriches your life, and aligns with your values and goals. The bottom-line goal of supporting your health in the occupational dimension is that you are sharing your gifts and talents with others in a rewarding and meaningful way. Paycheck not needed.

For those of you that are full-time students right now, you are working on preparing yourself for the occupational role in a meaningful way. You need to learn the skills, communication styles, responsibilities, and roles of the occupational pathway you are studying for. You do that in a meaningful way, like going to a technical college, trade school, university, or grad school. Or you could be taking a training program sponsored by your current or future employer to prepare you for the role. What about the stay-at-home mom or dad (hardest job in the world, by the way)? How do you support this dimension? Well, you are most certainly using your gifts and talents in a meaningful way to better the lives of your children and partner, and to operationally manage the household. Retired or disabled? Same thing goes for you all, too! What can you do to share your gifts and talents with others in a meaningful way? Volunteer in your community. Again, none of this has to be a "for pay" job to "get credit" for this dimension. Perhaps you were once a teacher but are now retired; you could volunteer at the local school helping kids that need that extra one-on-one time to learn how to read. Disabled? Maybe your talents lie in the arts. Can you volunteer at a local homeless shelter to work on arts and crafts with kids after school? Or go over to a neighbor's house to dog sit while they are on vacation? Let go of the notion that you need to get a paycheck every other Friday to be healthy and strong in your occupational dimension.

What about those folks that are working a "for pay" job? OK, let's take a look there, too. Do you find your work powerful and meaningful, and do you feel like you are part of a team that makes a difference? I am not talking about changing the world to make a difference or something powerful like an "I make six figures" kind of power job either. Let me share an example. At the beginning of my career, I was a nursing assistant. It is super hard work that can be deflating and depressing. It is physically back breaking and emotionally draining. But there were times when a resident would take my hand, look me in my eyes, and truly thank me for something as small as helping her to put a little blush on her cheeks. Or when a family member would hug me at the bedside of their dying mom. Or when the lady with end-stage dementia would smile in some sort of recognition when I knelt down to chat with her about the day. That was powerful, meaningful work that supported my occupational wellness.

Here are some other ways you might consider supporting your occupational dimension of health.

- Ensure your chosen occupation aligns with your values, passions, and strengths; if not, brainstorm pathways you can achieve this
- Find joy in your work or volunteerism, and share that joy with others around you
- Be a mentor to others at your workplace or your volunteerism location
- When in school, strive to actually learn, not just jump through hoops or earn "As"
- Seek internships and experiential opportunities to better appreciate the role of the job
- Seek continuing education opportunities offered by your employer or volunteerism location
- Talk with your supervisor about ways to improve in your current role or a pathway to a new role
- Go the "extra mile" to be exceptional, instead of just "meeting expectations"
- Take pride in your work and volunteerism
- Embrace a "continuous quality improvement" attitude in your job
- But still take some time to unplug and get away from the job (stay-at-home parents, I am for sure talking to you here!!)
- Have healthy boundaries and balance; know when to say "no" to avoid burnout

Now it's your turn! Tell me what your strengths and opportunities are in this dimension.

Strengths:

Opportunities:

Next up, I want you to write down one or two things that you might realistically be able to do in the next couple of months to support your occupational dimension of wellness. Just make sure that they are realistic for you to do.

Intervention(s):

The spiritual dimension has this connotation of required religiosity, and for those of you that ascribe to an institutionalized religion, that would be a correct assumption. However, for those of you that are "nones"—meaning you list "none" on forms asking you about your religious affiliation because you do not identify with a religion—please do not skip this conversation. About a third of Americans under the age of 30 are "nones," so there are a lot of you out there. Hang in there with me. There is a big difference between being religious and being spiritual that we will explore here. One can be religious and spiritual at the same time, religious but not spiritual, spiritual and not religious. Confused yet? Hold on. Let me explain.

Embracing the spiritual dimension of wellness basically means that you appreciate that there is a higher power than yourself. Now that could mean God, Allah, the Flying Spaghetti Monster,

Ganesh, Mother Nature, Mother Universe, or the global collective community as a whole. It means we are not alone. Having a connection to the power of life by some means is what supports the spiritual dimension. This connection gives you, the individual, a purpose and awareness of who you are, where you came from, why you are here, and an ethical compass to help you lead a values-based life. This is our pathway for humans to discover meaning and purpose in this life.

I feel "life" and "values-based decision making" are tossed around quite a bit, but what do those terms really mean? As applied to the spiritual dimension, this means living your faith, for real. There are many people out there that may appear to be devout religious or spiritual people, but their beliefs do not align with their actions. These folks may read their faith-based texts, attend weekly services, chat with others about their true path to enlightenment in this realm, and from the outside looking in, appear to be very much in line with their ascribed belief systems, but in reality their personal or professional choices do not align with their teachings. This causes conflict and weakness in this dimension. Here are some examples. A devout Catholic woman may assist her teenage daughter in securing birth control to prevent pregnancy outside of marriage. A Buddhist man's desire to climb the corporate ladder at every co-worker's expense causes him to hurt others around him, despite his belief in karma and how that will impact his future life. A person who claims to be an eco-environmentalist continues to purchase disposable, consumable items (those darn plastic forks keep popping back into our conversation) when it is inconvenient to use reusable items. These choices and actions are opposed to the individual's spiritual acumen, and only serve to diminish this dimension. Reflecting on your values doing a sort of "double-check system" when making life choices both big and small can help support this dimension.

Let's take a bit of time to really flesh out what your values actually are. I am going to have you complete a series of exercises to identify some core values you hold. It is going to be difficult because we all have a lot of things and ideas that we hold dear and value, but I am going to force you to whittle those down into a very small list. In this activity I would like you to write down the top 15 values from the list at the website below. You can also find the values list in the appendix on page 277.

To access the values list, scan the QR code with your phone or type bit.ly/3yLFeL6 into your browser.

Then whittle that list down to your top ten. Finally, choose your top five from those remaining. Now list your five top values here. Go ahead, write them down, including a note to yourself about why you chose these specific five values. We will come back to these later.

Value #1

Value #2

Value #3

Value #4

Value #5

When we have a strong spiritual dimension, we are more resilient to life changes and can approach them with a sense of positivity, knowing that there is a meaning to life that is larger than ourselves as individuals. Coming from this space of positivity and hope, we can employ a clearer sense of self-worth and inner peace; we can be more open to forgiveness both in ourselves and others, and we can be more accepting of difficult times, from the normal ups and downs of life to even death. In turn, this can help stave off the effects of stress, which can include anxiety, depression, and even physical illness. This directly ties into the work we have already put in surrounding the inner critic and flipping your switch to one of positivity as opposed to "Negative Nellie-ism." Starting to see how this work is all interconnected and interrelated?

Here are some other ways you might consider supporting your spiritual dimension of health, and some of these, as you will recall, were already discussed in setting your scene for behavior change (double dipping is great!).

- Meditate
- Embrace a daily gratitude practice
- Pray
- Hold a sense of appreciation as to how you fit into this world
- Be kind to the earth
- Seek the truth
- Stand up for what is true and just
- Live your values in your actions, not just in your words

Seek quiet time for self-reflection

Sit in nature

Employ values-based decision making for big and small choices

Hike

Forgive

Connect with others to talk about values and beliefs (those that have the same and differing ideas)

Hug a tree

Help others that are less fortunate than you are

Now it's your turn! Tell me what your strengths and opportunities are in this dimension.

Strengths:

_____

_____

_____

Opportunities:

_____

_____

_____

Next up, I want you to write down one or two things that you might realistically be able to do in the next couple of months to support your spiritual dimension of wellness. Just make sure that they are realistic for you to do.

Intervention(s):

_____

_____

_____

Next up is the social dimension! Please keep in mind that this is different from the social determinants of health. SDOH are all about "access to resources," whereas the social dimension of health is all about those marvelous relationships we talked about in Chapter

Four. The social dimension of wellness is about building and maintaining relationships with those close to you and those not so close. It means having a healthy relationship with your family, unicorns, and community folks, but also taking this one step further and being a good global citizen. It means that you are able to make connections with other human beings by establishing and maintaining positive relationships that are supportive and caring. To be supportive and caring, first start in your own home, neighborhood, and community. But then extend that to also be considerate of people that you might not ever get to meet: those that are living in war-torn or authoritarian countries (remember my Rick Steves Iran story), those that are making your jeans at the risk of their own health and the health of their waterways, and, generally speaking, those people that do not have their basic safety and security needs met around the globe.

I recently was scrolling through my social media feed and saw someone reaching out for help in a community forum. This person shared a story of depleted financial assets related to a medical issue, and they were not getting paid until the following week and were out of food. I live in a smaller community where the food banks are not open every day or even every week. I braced myself for rampant judgment in the comments section, but in turn I was amazed to see that not one person reacted negatively or assumed this person was "scamming." There was an outpouring of offerings to drop food and household necessities off for this person to get her through the week. She repeatedly stated she did not need much, just a bit to get her through the week, yet there was an outpouring of support. This is a great example of social wellness. Coming together for our fellow humans, building connections one person at a time, even if you don't know them.

I am not going to belabor this dimension because you have already read a chapter devoted to the importance of social relationships and how they truly make the world go around and support health. I will, however, mention some more of the health benefits of being a social critter. You see, humans were not meant to live alone, hidden away in little apartments, isolated from people in their community. While technically surrounded by other humans, we can still feel completely alone. There is a difference between being alone versus feeling lonely. Being alone is a physical state of being the only person present. Some people prefer this to being in crowds of people. Having alone time is not a bad thing; everyone needs it to rest, refocus, recuperate, and re-energize. But loneliness is the emotional state of feeling alone or disconnected from other humans. A person could have a lot of social contact but still feel lonely. And loneliness is not so good for your health. Certain groups of people are at higher risk for feelings of loneliness and social isolation. Older adults, LGBTQ people, minorities, and first-generation immigrants are at high risk of social isolation and its deleterious effects on health.

So why is this such a big deal? Well, because we know that feelings of loneliness and social isolation are associated with a higher risk of depression, anxiety, and suicide. I think most can see the connection here, but did you know that it also places a person at higher risk for physical problems? Yup, that's right, things like dementia, heart disease, and stroke are more likely to affect those that feel disconnected from other humans. It is probably due to the fact that those who feel disconnected often smoke, move less, and eat more poorly. More of those lifestyle choices that are not always choices. Think about this. The last time you broke up with a partner, had an argument with a friend, or felt left out of a group, did you crave comfort foods like potato chips and cookies? Or did you want to grill some chicken, chop some fresh kale, and make your own homemade vinaigrette for a lovely summer salad? I have a suspicion it was the former, not the latter. Did you feel like binge watching the latest romcom on Netflix? Or did you go for a five-mile power run? The former again? Yes, that is just human nature. When we feel sad or lonely, we tend to make choices that will soothe ourselves, like sitting on the couch and ordering in that garbage pizza. It's human nature and can be a vicious cycle. I don't know about you, but when I eat junky foods and feel all bloated, I have diminished motivation to get off the couch and engage in healthy behaviors. But on the flip side, when I am feeling good, out and about enjoying my community and my friendships, I am more likely to make that salad and go for a walk with my friends. It can be a feedback loop, for better or for worse.

Here is a great example of how a small intervention can be powerful in this dimension. Someone I know had a new neighbor, and this new neighbor just happened to be a first-generation immigrant. Unfamiliar with customs, laws, and language, I'm sure you can imagine it would be difficult to adjust, create social connectedness, and feel healthy in this dimension. This person invited her new neighbor over so that they could learn from each other. She asked the new neighbor to teach her how to make eggrolls and in return she taught her how to bake chocolate chip cookies. How great is that?!

I will give you a contrasting case study example to put the power of social connectedness into perspective. A young new mom brings her newborn home. She lives in her apartment in New York City, without a partner or family close by to stop in and check on her. She is off of work for six weeks since she just had the baby. She lives alone with thousands of people surrounding her, but yet is isolated from true human connection. You can see how this is just setting this new mom up for heartache and poor health, right? On the flip side, imagine a new mom with strong social connections. Folks from her church sign up for a meal train, so they take turns stopping by each evening to drop off a casserole and coo over the new babe, imparting their birthing stories and helpful hints on parenting. Her mom stops by to cheerlead when breastfeeding feels just too tough to continue. A friend watches the baby while the new mom takes a 20-minute bath to soothe her bottom and just emotionally check out for a bit. This mom is far more likely to rebound from the trauma of birth faster, have a lesser risk of postpartum depression, and continue to breastfeed, which sets the stage for a healthy mom and a healthy baby presently and also in years to come. You see, we were not meant to be trapped in small little boxes, isolated from human connection. We are healthier and happier together. You reap what you sow. Sow seeds of connection!

Here are some other ways you might consider supporting your social dimension of health.

Volunteer

Play cards with a friend

Talk to your neighbor

Reach out to an old friend

Have a "pen pal"

Unplug

Say good morning to a stranger on the sidewalk

Join a group with those that have similar interests as you

Host an international student

Smile at people when you are running errands

Ask for help when you need it

Offer to help others when they might need it

Carpool for your children's activities

Hold the door for the person behind you

Visit with nursing home residents

Thank people

Be kind to customer service reps

Practice what you learned from *Sesame Street*

Now it's your turn! Tell me what your strengths and opportunities are in this dimension.

Strengths:

Opportunities:

Next up, I want you to write down one or two things that you might realistically be able to do in the next couple of months to support your social dimension of wellness. Just make sure that they are realistic for you to do.

Intervention(s):

_____

_____

_____

The emotional dimension is the next item to discuss. Emotional wellness translates to being able to understand and respect your feelings and the feelings of others; being able to effectively communicate those feelings and managing those feelings in a constructive manner. One last part of emotional wellness is seeing things through a positive lens. Hmmmm, I believe we have chatted about this before, too! Positivity is key to emotional well-being because when you can see things through that growth mindset and appreciate that even though things may seem lousy right now, we can probably find some way of appreciating their importance later in our life. Maybe not right now, but at some point, we will be able to reflect back on the importance and how that helped to shape and guide who you are today. One of my favorite sayings is, "Happiness is free for the taking, please help yourself." Please do so, my friends.

By embracing positivity and effectively communicating, managing, and regulating our emotions, we can support resilience against chronic stress. Stress is a killer. For real. Stress causes inflammation in the body; systemic, generalized inflammation. We know that activation of stress responses and chronic stress is linked to about three quarters of human diseases; these have been termed "stress-related disease." The most common stress-related diseases include cardiovascular diseases like hypertension and atherosclerosis, metabolic diseases such as diabetes and nonalcoholic fatty liver disease, neurological disorders such as depression and dementia, and cancer. Now I would like you to take an inventory of your stress levels. Stress is something that is very subjective, so this is not just about checking boxes of events or things that have happened, but more about your perception of your own stress levels. Complete the stress inventory below and calculate your score. Write that down and reflect on what that means to you personally.

To access the stress inventory scale, scan the QR code with your phone or type bit.ly/30D521Q into your browser.

When the body responds to stress, certain chemicals are released and certain physiological responses begin, things like an elevated heart rate and blood pressure. This happens during acute, or short-term, stress, which is not a bad thing. Acute stress keeps us on our toes so that we can do well on a test, be alert in heavy traffic, or perform well during an interview for a new job. But these physiological responses that occur day in and day out create a chronic stress response that is quite unhealthy. Chronic stress can inhibit our brain function, our normal body processes, and our immune system function. Remember the ACEs we talked about earlier? This is why kids with ACEs tend to have a higher likelihood of disease. To control inflammation, we need to control chronic stress. To control chronic stress, we need to support our emotional dimension of wellness.

A great way to support our emotional dimension is through getting adequate and quality sleep. Easier said than done, right? Here are some facts to lay the groundwork. Most Americans get less than seven hours of sleep a night, on average 6.7 hours. The recommendation by the American Psychological Association is – seven to nine hours per night for adults, and more for kiddos. Not only are Americans not getting enough sleep, almost half report crappy sleep, rating it as only "fair to poor." Here is the thing, when people don't sleep enough or don't sleep well, it causes stress. And guess what happens when people report increased stress? Yup. They don't sleep so well. This feeds a disastrous sleep/stress cycle that is really difficult to break.

You may be thinking, "Yeah, I can totally run on five hours a sleep a night and I am just fine." Why is this sleep thing so important? Great question. Well, when you sleep poorly or not enough, a few things happen. Sure, you might feel a little bit sluggish or even lazy, but more importantly, not only does stress increase, but so does your inability to cope with future stressors. You become more irritable, have trouble concentrating, and are more sad or even depressed. I don't know about you, but if I am having a hard time sleeping, I am far more likely to break down crying or to throw a tantrum than if I had a good night's sleep under my belt. This is called emotional lability—vast mood swings or an exaggeration of emotions or feelings that are expressed greater than the extent of what would be a "normal" reaction—and it is caused by lack of sleep and stress, among other things. In other words, overreacting. And overreacting typically does not support social connectedness and positive relationships.

You can see how this lack of sleep and increased stress in turn can hurt you in terms of human connectedness and relationships (social dimension of wellness), but it also affects your ability to focus and your memory capacity (intellectual dimension of wellness). You will have an increased risk of accidents (physical dimension), and it significantly impacts your emotional wellness, too. This sleep/stress issue sort of has cascading effects, doesn't it? These are the more short-term issues of that nefarious sleep/stress cycle that I just listed, but what does it do to you in the long run? Obesity, high blood pressure, impaired glucose tolerance (which can result in diabetes), chemical dependence, cardiovascular disease, and shortened lifespan result from stress and poor sleep, just to name a few. Not good stuff.

Here are some other ways, aside from getting good sleep, that you might consider in supporting your emotional dimension of health.

> Acknowledge your feelings
>
> Talk about your feelings
>
> Communicate your needs (I live by the adage "when you ask for what you want, you up the chances of getting it"—and it often works!)
>
> Accept disappointment with grace and humility (common humanity)
>
> Support others when they stumble (common humanity)
>
> Respond, don't react (mindfulness)
>
> Reflect before you respond (aka think before you speak)

Acknowledge the feelings of those around you (active listening and healthy relationship characteristic)

Accept what you're feeling (this doesn't mean you need to act on the feelings, but accept them instead of pushing them away)

Embrace a positive attitude

Harness a growth mindset

Cultivate and maintain relationships

Meditate

Employ stress management activities like exercising and managing healthy boundaries

Practice self-care activities that work for you (take a bath, read a book, get a massage)

Practice mindfulness

Listen to your narrator and calm your inner critic

Laugh

Smile

Remember your gratitude practice

I think you can see that many of these interventions can have impactful results on more than just one dimension of wellness. What a bargain, right?!

Now it's your turn! Tell me what your strengths and opportunities are in this dimension.

Strengths:

_____

_____

_____

Opportunities:

_____

_____

_____

Next up, I want you to write down one or two things that you might realistically be able to do in the next couple of months to support your emotional dimension of wellness. Just make sure that they are realistic for you to do.

> Intervention(s):
>
> _____
>
> _____
>
> _____

The environmental dimension is next! We have already discussed the environmental determinants of health earlier, which by all means do have some overlap with this dimension, but I wanted to clarify the nuanced differences right up front. The environmental determinants include our natural and built environment and how they impact health outcomes, like the buildings we live in, the green spaces that surround us, etc. These are those larger scope environmental issues that are often influenced by governmental, corporate, and political systems. The environmental determinants are things like what chemicals are approved by the EPA to spray on our farm fields, and the building of water systems that are free of lead pipes for our cities, or having sidewalks and streetlights to light our path and afford a safe evening walk in our neighborhood, or who has access to water rights during droughts. The environmental dimension of wellness has a more personal influence by way of taking on a personal responsibility for environmental stewardship and developing a personalized connection to nature. To impact the environmental determinants, we can use our purchasing power and the power of voting to influence those systems and policy level changes. In the environmental dimension of wellness, I will ask you to recognize your own responsibility for the quality of the air, the water, and the land, and try to make a positive impact on the quality of our environment through our daily choices and our buying power.

The first topic we need to address when considering our strengths and opportunities in the environmental dimension is that we are woefully lacking in time spent outdoors. This can lead to physical problems like obesity, as well as mental, spiritual, and emotional challenges throughout the lifespan. Something to consider: children today are only spending a total of four to seven minutes outdoors each day. You heard me right. Four to seven minutes. Without outdoor time, how can children grow to feel a sense of connectedness to Mother Nature, appreciate its health benefits, understand the wonder of wildlife, be advocates against pollution, or support the various dimensions of wellness and just value nature in general? By contrast, according to the American Academy of Child and Adolescent Psychiatry, kids in the United States ages eight to twelve spend four to six hours a day watching or using screens, and teens spend up to nine hours. This could be a canary in the mineshaft. With so many children spending so little time with Mother Nature, what will their choices be as grown-ups? Will they choose to preserve nature's beauty and wonder if they never learned to appreciate it in the first place? This disconnection to our environment places conservation efforts and our natural resources at risk. This has a term associated with it as well: it has been coined "nature deficit disorder." While this is not a medically diagnosable disorder, it does signify the impact of this disconnection.

Why is it so important to love Mother Nature? As I mentioned earlier, connecting with nature can have spiritual wellness benefits.

But what else? It also supports our social, emotional, and physical wellness as well! Talk about bang for your buck! Connecting with Mother Nature increases our awe and wonderment of life, supports generalized positive emotions by releasing certain "happy" chemicals, has a calming effect, boosts your gratitude practice, and supports your spiritual dimension by connecting to something larger than the self. It helps neighborhoods decrease temperatures, reduce crime, and increase social cohesion. It reduces stress hormones, encourages physical activity, and reduces blood pressure, heart rate, and muscle tension. That is a lot of goodness!

Forest bathing is a great intervention to help support your wellness in this dimension. You heard me right, forest bathing. Yes, it actually is a real thing. Forest bathing is not just going for a hike in the woods; rather it is about taking your time, being mindful, wandering in nature with no apparent goal. Using the mindfulness techniques you already learned about, you can stop to soak up all of the data your senses are offering you while wandering about. Hear the rustle of the wind through the leaves. Feel the rough bark and smooth leaves on the trees. Feel and hear the crunch of stones under your feet. Smell the apple trees in bloom. Breathe it in. Breathe it out. Bathe in Mother Nature's wonder. Be present. This practice can boost your immunity and lower blood pressure by reducing the release of stress hormones. Gotta love nature!

Not only do limited and loose connections to Mother Nature negatively impact our environmental dimension of wellness, but as you will recall, the environmental determinants can as well. Recall that the environmental determinants are those social, political, and economic systems. The environmental dimension of wellness includes our individual choices that influence and are influenced by those systems. They are interrelated and interdependent. Pollution in our home, community, and global environment are as well. Our homes and the water coming into our homes can be polluted with toxic chemicals from fertilizer runoff, lead in old pipes, household cleaning products, mold, and insecticides. Pollution in the community can affect air quality, land, and waterways. Air pollution like smog, fumes from cars and industry, and even indoor air pollutants like radon impact health by increasing the likelihood of lung damage, resulting in diseases like asthma and cancer. Land pollution occurs when chemicals from landfills, generalized chemical use, agricultural waste runoff, and even air pollutants like auto exhaust settle or leach into the soil. Clearly this is a problem, since we tend to grow vegetables in soil and the earth and water have a reciprocal cleaning agreement. Finally, water pollution occurs from many of these same items that I have listed already, but is also impacted by rising temperatures, which react with the pollutants. For example, agricultural runoff into freshwater lakes and streams coupled with rising temperatures increases the likelihood of algal blooms, which in turn kills ecosystems within the waterways. These are just a handful of ways that pollutants affect our well-being.

Our intrinsic human need to connect with nature for the betterment of our health is placed at risk when the environment itself is at risk from various types of pollution. Even though environmental hazards can feel overwhelming or make us feel like the situation is hopeless, keep in mind that there are many interventions that you as an individual can take to support environmental wellness. Every little bit helps!

Here are some other ways beside forest bathing that you might consider supporting your environmental dimension of health.

Buy local

Reduce, reuse, and recycle

Choose plant-based cleaning products

Pick up litter in your neighborhood when you see it, or go for "clean-up hikes" to pick up litter in your community or on nature trails

Choose organic food items or grow the food yourself without chemicals

Don't put fertilizer or other chemicals on your lawn

Take your lawn out and replace it with a pollinator garden

Fix leaky pipes and faucets

Push mow, like the good old-fashioned push mower with rotating blades!

Purchase meats from small farms as opposed to factory farms

Hunt to source your own local meat

Eat less animal-based protein; try "meatless Mondays"

Take children outdoors

Walk in the grass in your bare feet

Open the windows and shut off the air conditioner

Hug trees

Drive less, walk or bike more

Carpool

Compost

Eat less

Generally speaking, just try to have a smaller footprint on this earth based on all of your purchases

Now it's your turn! Tell me what your strengths and opportunities are in this dimension.

Strengths:

___

___

___

Opportunities:

___

___

___

Next up, I want you to write down one or two things that you might realistically be able to do in the next couple of months to support your environmental dimension of wellness. Just make sure that they are realistic for you to do.

Intervention(s):

_____

_____

_____

And last but most certainly not least is the physical dimension—probably what most of you have been waiting for. Sorry, I have one more "but wait" before we discuss this dimension. The reason I left this dimension for last is not because I was "saving the best for last" or trying to get you to read more before you put the book down. No folks, it's because if you take care of the stuff in the other dimensions first, you are more likely to be successful in sustained behavior change in this dimension. Remember my panic attack issue? Well, I had tried to lose weight and get in shape plenty of times prior to my work on the panic attack problem, but you know what? I couldn't make those changes stick because my head just wasn't in the game. I had too many other unhealthy issues in other dimensions that would get in the way and become barriers, and ultimately those all conspired to set me up for failure in sustainable behavior change in the physical dimension. The panic attacks were just a symptom of a larger issue, not the issue itself. I had to learn how to stop, slow down, be mindful, understand what health really is, tame my inner critic, and switch my frame of mind to one of positivity to be able to consistently move more, eat less, and treat my body the way it deserves to be treated. And voila! I am the lightest weight and the healthiest I have ever been—even including my teenage years! For me, that "head stuff" had to come first to lay the foundation for success.

Now I am not saying you can't make sustainable physical changes stick on their own; you very well might be able to. But I am saying it will be easier in the long run for you to start with the other stuff first. Let me again use some examples to clarify my point that if there are concerns in other dimensions of wellness, barriers will inherently pop up to get in the way of the interventions you want to embrace in the physical dimension of wellness.

Case scenario: I want to eat healthier and work out five days per week so I can lose 15 pounds.

- Financial dimension is out of balance. If you are not financially comfortable, you may have to depend on food banks, which most often offer highly processed, high-calorie, low-nutrient-dense foods. You may not have the extra finances to purchase a pair of tennis shoes to safely or comfortably work out in, you might not be able to afford a gym membership, or you may live in a neighborhood that is not safe to work out or go for walks in.
- Intellectual dimension is out of balance. If you do not have a curiosity about how to move safely during a new exercise

routine, or to explore ways to cook foods in different ways that are healthy for you, then you more than likely will not investigate these thoroughly or in a manner in which you will find success in your goal.
- Occupational dimension is out of balance. If you are working 60+ hours per week at your job plus trying to juggle kids and manage a household, you might not have the time, stamina, or emotional capacity to add a workout regimen or to avoid ordering takeout when you are exhausted. Your motivation to change may be there at the beginning, but will quickly fade when the realities of life get in the way; like, there isn't enough time in the day to work that much, take care of my familial responsibilities, take time to work out, and do meal prep on top of all the other stuff.
- Spiritual dimension is out of balance. If you do not see yourself as part of a larger whole spiritually, within your community, or within the global community, or if you have an unclear sense of your purpose, then what is the point or motivation in losing 15 pounds?
- Social dimension is out of balance. Having few or strained relationships, and not having a friend to exert positive peer pressure for healthy habits, can cause stress and isolation, which may support continued physical inactivity and poor eating habits.
- Emotional dimension is out of balance. You may not be sleeping well or sleeping enough, which in turn increases stress. Increased stress increases the secretion of hormones that in turn increase the likelihood of eating "comfort foods" and feeling too overwhelmed to be physically active.
- Environmental dimension is out of balance. You may be living in an area that lacks green space or has poor air quality related to pollution. Exercising outside may be hazardous

to your health. Your indoor air quality may be poor due to mold and radon, making it difficult to breathe while you work out indoors or exacerbating a chronic illness that you already have, making it more difficult and uncomfortable to be physically active.

You can see how when we don't have our other dimensions in order, it will certainly strain our physical dimension in so many different capacities. These dimensions are all interrelated. They all "pull and tug" on one another, either negatively or positively.

Now that we have that out of the way, let's jump into this feet first! My message is super simple. Eat less. Avoid fake foods as much as possible, especially sugar. Move more. Are you ready to scream yet? Sorry. I know you might have been looking for a magic bullet, but this book is not that. You have stuck with me this far; please hang on with me just a little bit longer. I am going to go over some guidelines for you. And I promise you, if you follow them, you will feel better. You may lose some weight. You may gain some lean muscle mass. But that is not the point of all of this. Remember that person that met me on the street and said, "You look so joyful!"? Integrating these things in your life will transform your human form into one that sends that message outwardly to others and, more importantly, to yourself. Even if you have disabilities, challenges, mobility limitations, pain, or any other self-limiting ideations, doing these things to the best of your ability can help minimize these things and maximize your true potential. In the end, these interventions will help you to cherish the body that you have been given in all of its infinite glory, and to be grateful for everything it does for you every minute of every day. It is easy to think about the body part that gives you grief, either because of pain, disability, lackluster functioning, or internal self-consciousness, but when we are going through this dimension, try to focus on all of the amazing things your body does for you every moment of every day. From the act of breathing without even thinking about it, to the ability of purposeful movement in scratching your dog's belly, to seeing the smile on the face of a loved one when you enter the room. Appreciate all those miraculous functions that are so often overlooked.

OK, here we go, first step. Eat less. Americans today eat way more than they have in the past. One reason is because food is just so readily available. We talked about food deserts and food swamps earlier in relation to the social determinants of health. Food deserts are geographical areas where there is limited access to supermarkets and a higher percentage of economically disadvantaged folks living nearby. Supermarkets tend to not take up shop in places where the communities are poor. Therefore, people are forced to shop in small stores with expensive and limited supplies (bodegas and gas stations) or access food from food pantries. Food deserts and food swamps often go hand in hand. Food swamps are condensed geographical areas that support an obesogenic environment, meaning you are more likely to be obese if you live in the area. Ever drive down a stretch of city street or highway and see fast-food restaurant after fast-food restaurant, metro marts selling a baker's dozen of donuts for a few bucks, and convenience stations selling 128-ounce Slurpees for a buck, all lined up in a row for us to belly up to the buffet at? These are food swamp areas. These food swamps actually can predict obesity greater than food deserts. The foods in these swamps are mass produced, readily accessible, nutrient poor, calorie dense, and cheap. These types of foods can also be addictive to some people.

The next problem is that food sizes have exponentially expanded over the last several decades. This is known as "portion distortion." A bagel just a couple of decades ago was on average 140 calories and three inches in diameter. You know where I am going with this. Today that "normal"-sized bagel is on average 350 calories and six inches in diameter. An average cheeseburger 20 years ago was about 330 calories. Today the average burger is about 590 calories. And remember, that is just an average. The "Ultimate Cheeseburger" from Jack in the Box is 840 calories. A "Baconator" from Wendy's is 940 calories, and a "Monster Thickburger" from Hardee's is a whopping 1,300 calories. That's about how many calories I should be taking in in one day. Throw in a large Coke and fries, and you have yourself a banner day. And who knows, I might need to finish that off with a cookie the size of my head. Really, why do we need cookies the size of our head? Let me offer you a piece of advice. If a food item is as large as a body part, you might want to take a hard pass on that. Have I eaten enough cookies to total the size of my head in one sitting? Absolutely, yes, many times. Why? Why is it that we have this desire to eat more than we really need? Again, we can look to evolution. When food is available we eat it, because it might not be available tomorrow. Well, just like those saber-toothed cats, we don't need to worry about food scarcity anymore, because as you can see, calories are readily available everywhere you look. Combine evolution with a complete perversion of what food actually is by way of junk calories, and it is a combination for loosening the belt more and more.

Calories are everywhere. Check. We have that established. Next up, they are easy to access. Check, got that too. Going back to that food desert discussion once more, remember we talked about the two-pound bag of pretzels instead of the overpriced and overripe produce? OK, let's take that one step further. Those junk calories are easily accessible because they are shelf stable. Manufacturers use chemicals and preservatives to make sure that these foods can sit on a shelf and not go bad for ages. That increases their profit margin. Ever notice the bagel at your local mom-and-pop bakery lasts about a day before you might chip a tooth on it, but the bagel you buy in a five-pack at the grocery store seems to last for weeks? There's a reason for that. It increases the manufacturer's profit margin to pump it with preservatives to be able to sit on a shelf that long. So, when you go to the supermarket, there are rows and rows and rows of shelf stable food items. Why? Because people are making money off of your health. And most often these foods are less expensive than fresh foods. Why? Because the fresh foods go bad more quickly! This is why it is less expensive to shop in the interior of the grocery store as opposed to the perimeter of the grocery stores, where you will find the bakery, meat, produce, and dairy departments. Not only do we have shelf stable foods that last forever (yes, I think Twinkies will actually outlive the apocalypse, based on the number of chemicals in those dreamy little cakes), but we have access to those foods 24/7. You can wake up at 2 am craving M&Ms, drive down to the local supermarket, gas station, metro mart, take your pick, and grab a bag of those little gems. Not only can you grab a bag of them, but you can grab a one-pound bag of them. Because everyone knows if one ounce is good, one pound is fantastic.

Calories are everywhere and easy to access, yes and yes, we have that covered. However, food is readily available not only because of these aforementioned issues, but because this actually reflects our societal norms, too. Think about what happens when someone passes away. You take the family a casserole (showing my Midwestern roots here). When you have a birthday party, what do you do? Eat cake and ice cream together. Go to a friend's house for cocktails? There's finger food waiting for you. Go to a wedding? Get a free meal. Kids have a soccer match? Better pack snacks. Road trips with the fam require Bugles so you can put them on your fingertips and pretend you are a witch. You get the idea. It doesn't matter what we are doing; as humans, when we gather, we tend to share food. When we sat around the fire picking mastodon meat out of our teeth, it was a thing, too. That is just our human nature as social critters.

Next up, we need to talk about what types of foods you eat. When I say eat less to stay healthy in this dimension, it is not about losing weight (although that may be a consequence of this); it is more about how to properly fuel your body with the foods it actually needs to stay in a state of health and avoid developing chronic disease. You may have heard "calories in versus calories out" before. You may have heard that a calorie is a calorie, no matter what vehicle it is using to transport itself inside your mouth. Well, soda, candy, and junk food companies probably want you to believe that, but it is just not true. We need to look at nutritional value and food's impact on our body and brains here. If you eat 400 calories of Ho Hos as opposed to 400 calories of salmon, you are going to spike your blood sugar, rev your pancreas, light up dopamine levels in your brain, and cause chemicals in your gut to tell your brain you need more of that sugary goodness as often as you can get your hands on it. Oh, and get zero real nutrition to actually fuel your body's cells in the process. The more you eat those Ho Hos, the more you crave them. Positive feedback loop again. A calorie is not a calorie.

Not only do processed foods have those chemicals and preservatives in them to keep them shelf stable through the apocalypse, but most have hidden sugar, too. If you go back into that supermarket, three quarters of all the packaged foods in there have added sugar in them in one form or another. Many times, manufacturers are sneaky about it using names that you wouldn't think would be bad for you, like rice syrup, agave nectar, or barley malt. There are currently 61 different names that you will find on food labels that are used to hide sugar in your foods. Make no mistake, these are still sugars. They are tricky not only with the names, but how they package and market products, too. A berry yogurt parfait sounds pretty healthy for breakfast, right? And it will definitely tell you that on the package, but really, not so much. It is one big, processed sugar bomb.

The American Heart Association recommends that women should have no more than 6 teaspoons or 25 grams of added sugar per day, men no more than 9 teaspoons or 38 grams per day, and kiddos should have no more than 3 to 6 teaspoons or 12 to 25 grams per day. Check out your favorite container of yogurt the next time you are at the store. It will probably have about 20 to 30 grams of sugar in it. Throw some granola and syrupy fruit on that bad boy parfait, and you have totally blown your sugar allotment out of the water for the day. And many people eat this for breakfast thinking it is a healthy option. It is a lie, my friends. Don't buy into it. Look at yogurt marketed to kids, and you will see an even more egregious amount of sugar. Now, the takeaway should NOT be that yogurt is inherently bad. You can buy plain yogurt, add real fruit to the top of it along with a drizzle of honey or maple syrup, and have a nice, slightly sweetened breakfast without making your poor little pancreas weep.

Just to be clear, I am not just picking on yogurt here. I am an equal opportunity sugar cynic. Cereals are another big offender. First, most of us suffer from portion distortion (as I spoke about earlier) when it comes to cereal. I myself feel as though one bowl is one serving; however, my bowl is often filled with about three cups of cereal with milk splashing over the side as I carry it over to the couch where I can watch the latest sci-fi Netflix original, binging on sugar while lying to myself that I am being healthy . . . sorry, got sidetracked there for a minute. One serving most often is anywhere from one to one and a half cups of cereal. I think we have established that that is absolutely ridiculous. That's like eating nine potato chips—it just can't happen. Even "healthy cereals" are just loaded with sugar. Let's use my favorite couch cereal, Raisin Bran, as an example here. One serving of this tasty treat is one cup. You all know that I eat three cups in one sitting (not counting milk at all here, just the straight-up cereal). There are 17 grams of sugar in one cup of cereal, so I am eating 51 grams of sugar during the first ten minutes of *Vampire Diaries* (don't judge me). OK, that makes me feel gross just thinking about it. Want me to gross you out even more? Think about sitting down and putting 12 teaspoons of sugar in my mouth in one sitting. No one would ever do that, right?! But that is literally what I am doing while I am zoning out watching Elena and Damon trying to catch a werewolf. Want to be grossed out one more time? Answer this question. How many pounds of added sugar do Americans consume each year? That's right, I said that correctly. Pounds. How many pounds? The answer? Sit down. Fifty-seven. *Dios mío.*

Why am I making such a huge deal about sugar? Let's talk about that. You see, sugar doesn't just make you add pounds, it makes you sick. It is actually as toxic to the liver as alcohol. Can you imagine giving your kids some beer at dinnertime to wash down their chicken? Absolutely not, but we have no thoughts about offering a Powerade with a sidecar of cookies for being a member of the clean plate club. Here is what happens when we eat too much sugar. We can develop fatty liver disease, which typically used to only be seen in alcoholics. Now we can see this in children and have given it a new name, nonalcoholic fatty liver disease; hence you can see that it is certainly not from giving them alcohol. Sugar consumption has also been linked to obesity, inflammatory disorders, metabolic syndrome, cardiovascular disease, diabetes, and dementia. This is serious stuff that is literally hiding in plain sight as most of us eat too much of it on a daily basis. And remember, it's tricky. I am not just talking to the person that drinks soda every day. One sandwich on whole-wheat bread can account for 2 grams of sugar just from the bread. Doesn't sound like a lot, but it adds up quickly when you account for all of your other food items in the daily total. Two tablespoons of French dressing on your salad has about 5 grams (and who really only puts two tablespoons of dressing on a salad anyway?). A glass of almond milk has 7 grams. A serving of spaghetti sauce has about 10 grams. Chocolate milk has about 24 grams. Who's tallying this up? We don't need to, we all know it's just too much.

And if you think that you are doing yourself a favor by using artificial sweeteners, think again. They are worse than real sugar. Here is what happens when you use the fake stuff. You ingest this sweet stuff, your brain thinks "Oh wow, we have a ton of sugar coming on board, let's dump a whole lot of insulin out there to control it!", and then the sugar doesn't come. Your brain gets confused and says, "But we dumped all these great hormones out there to take care of that sugar dump, where did it go? You need to eat more, man. Eat. Eat. Eat!" You are hungrier when you use these artificial sweeteners and therefore you eat more. So that diet cola is not saving you calories, but revving your brain to make yo-yo hormone dumps and to make you crave more calories. Leave it in the store. Don't bring it home.

If added sugar is in three quarters of processed foods, even those that are savory, and you know that added sugar most definitely does not do a body good, then what do you do? Here is the key. Eat. Real. Food. Things without a barcode. Things that you can't keep in your pantry to see if they will outlast the next *Star Wars* movie. Things you need to put in your refrigerator. I know it is easier said than done. But the more you can put into your mouth that is real food and not a perverted version of calories, the better you will feel and the more likely it is you will remain healthy. Real food contains the nutrients your body needs. And if you do this, you are also more likely to lose weight if you are above where you should be, and also gain more lean tissues in the process, because you will be giving your body the nutrients it actually needs not just to survive, but to thrive.

Ever hear of skinny fat? Or a malnourished obese person? These terms seem counterintuitive, but this is what our food system has created. People that may have a normal BMI (more on that bugaboo in a bit) but have a percentage of body fat that is too high and a lean muscle mass that is too low are coined "skinny fat." A malnourished obese person consumes excess calories but does not ingest the nutrients needed for normal cell function because the foods that are consumed are calorie rich and nutrient poor, hence malnourished, but overweight or obese. We need to flip the scenario to one in which a person is consuming foods that are nutrient rich and calorie poor. Things like vegetables, fruits, whole grains in their original states, nuts, and lean protein sources. In doing so, you will be healthier. What does healthier mean? You will be more able to combat acute illnesses, limit inflammation, stave off chronic illness, have less pain, and have a healthy, functioning gut. I get it, this is super difficult. Some of us have sugar addictions. Some of us really are passionate about sweet treats (for example, I have a strong love of chocolate-caramel-candy goodness), but sugar intake can be limited by reading labels and avoiding foods that are a trigger for you. I know that these chocolate goodies are my Achilles' heel, so I don't bring them home from the grocery store; then it is not a temptation.

I want to look at a couple of different measures before we move on to the movement part of this discussion. First off, the body mass index, otherwise known as **BMI**. You know I have issues with a handful of words. Well, this is one I take issue with too, simply because it really doesn't give us too much information about the health status of a person. However, every time you go into the clinic to see your medical provider, this is what they give you in terms of feedback on your weight. So I will start here. BMI is antiquated. It was created back in the 1800s, so it's kind of ridiculous that we are still using this, right? And it was created by a mathematician, not a physician. It does not take into account the distribution of fat, bone structure, or the amount of muscle a person has. It is just a set of averages to compare people against. Overall, it can be good to know your number, but don't hang your hat on this one when you go in for your checkup.

Next up is the belly to height ratio and the belly to hip ratio. For the belly to height ratio, you simply measure your belly at the midpoint (your natural waist) and figure out your height in inches and then divide. If a person is 5 feet 7 inches tall and has a waist measurement of 30, I would divide 30 by 67 to get a total of 0.44. The goal is to have a belly to height ratio that is less than 0.5. In this scenario the person is less likely to develop chronic illnesses such as diabetes or have cardiovascular problems. Next up is the belly to hip ratio. Measure your natural waist at the midpoint of your belly once again and then measure your hips at the widest part, around your bottom. Take those two numbers and divide them. If a person has a waist measurement of 32 and a hip measurement of 36, I would divide the two like this: 32/36, and I would get the number 0.89. Ranges for this calculation are broken down into low, moderate, and high-risk categories. You can see based on the chart that as a woman, this person would have a higher risk of developing chronic illnesses like diabetes and cardiovascular disease. Here is the chart for that:

Waist-to-hip ratio chart

Health risk	Women	Men
Low	0.80 or lower	0.95 or lower
Moderate	0.81–0.85	0.96–1.0
High	0.86 or higher	1.0 or higher

These tools are more sensitive than BMI because they account for body fat distribution, meaning where the body fat is located. It is more dangerous from a health perspective to carry your weight around your center than to carry it in your arms, thighs, and bottom. That is why it is important to appreciate distribution percentages in relation to weight risk. There are other tools that can give us an even better indication of the likelihood of developing chronic illness, but those include drawing labs and looking at blood work. I wanted to chat about these measures because they are sensitive to indicating a level of risk, yet are free and easy to do in the privacy of your own home, right here, right now. Seriously. Do that right here, right now, and write your numbers in.

Belly to height ratio:

_____

Belly to hip ratio:

_____

Bottom line: you don't need crazy diets. Just eat a reasonable amount of actual, real food. On a side note, eating less, especially less processed foods, impacts our environmental dimension by reducing our footprint, too, so you get a two-fer deal here. Who really wants chemicals and preservatives anyway, am I right?

Next up is moving more. Again, easier said than done, but there are some good life hacks we can embrace to do this and sneak it into our everyday lives. Remember how we talked about the differences in how much we are eating today compared to a couple of generations ago? The same thing holds true for how much we move, but in reverse. Think about this. Grandma had to actually sweep the house with a broom and dustpan; no Roomba for her. We had to drive cars with a standard transmission and no cruise control. We actually had to hand-wash clothes and dishes and trim the lawn edges with little scissor-like contraptions instead of that gas-powered weed whacker. When the phone rang, we actually had to get up off the couch and walk to the wall-mounted phone to answer it (sometimes we even had to run to answer the call if we thought it might be an important one). All of our modern conveniences have stolen precious physical movement moments in our daily lives. You might be thinking, washing dishes doesn't really add up to calorie burns, Carrie, but I promise, these "micro-movement interventions" really do add up over the course of the day. These little life hacks that I am offering in this section might not seem like a lot, but once you start to embrace the micro-movement intervention philosophy in your daily life, it can be impactful. What matters is movement. Bottom line: keep your body in motion as much as possible throughout the day.

First things first, though, we need to talk about what you should be doing each week in terms of your movement guidelines. If you are not here, yet, great, no worries; take baby steps to increase what you are doing when you can (more life hacks). If you are already doing these things, that's great, too. Keep doing them or try to do more. You can embrace the life hacks, too. There are four components to physical health as it relates to movement, and those include cardiorespiratory (cardio), strength training (don't get scared here, it will be OK; this does not require throwing iron around in a gym, I promise), flexibility (my other Achilles' heel), and balance training.

Cardiorespiratory exercise is anything that increases your heart and breathing rates. These can be things like biking, walking, and running, which are the usual suspects, but can also include things like vacuuming, raking, gardening, and push-mowing the lawn. Depending on the level of your cardio fitness right now, gardening may increase your heart rate and breathing rate, which can qualify as cardio exercise. Great news, right?! Yes. Movement is key here. Any kind of movement. If your main movement is getting up from the couch to grab a beer from the fridge, then let's set a goal of walking to the end of your driveway once a day, then twice a day, then three times a day; you get the idea. Seriously, I cannot stress enough that any kind of movement spaced throughout the day is what you need to do.

Micro-movement life hack #1: Earlier when we were talking about the dreaded processed food stuff, you may have been thinking to yourself, yeah, but cooking takes time and effort. Things like grocery shopping all the way around the perimeter of the store and not just up and down a couple of the aisles, and putting those groceries away, and then chopping all of that produce, and then meal prepping, cooking, packing up leftovers, washing dishes, putting the dishes away, ARGH . . . that is a lot of work. Well, guess what, that is all movement, too. Sneaky little bits here and there that you normally would not be getting if you ordered a pizza using your cell phone while sitting on the couch watching *Xena: Warrior Princess*, right? Right. Here is the deal. I know this stuff takes time. Start small, maybe one meal a week, and then one meal every other day, and then one meal every day that you prepare yourself with real foods. Small changes, whatever you can manage, will pay off over time. And your health is worth the investment of that time. It will give you more time in terms of greater life expectancy and a better quality of life with that additional time you have here on earth . . . what a great return on investment! Well, would you lookie here, here is the cheerleader coming out in me. You got this! You can do it! Yes, you can! This is guideline number one: move more and sit less. People who move more and sit less are healthier. Period.

Micro-movement life hack #2: Use your phone to count your steps. A good way to move more and sit less is to keep a keen eye on how many steps you are taking per day. Everyone says to aim for 10,000 steps a day, but that number is not really founded in research. It originally sprung from a device that was created and marketed in Japan in the 1960s and it sort of just "stuck." It can be a good goal to embrace, though. The latest research seems to indicate that if you hit the 7,500 step per day mark, you have a marked decrease in your mortality risk. However, more is better (up to a certain breakeven point). So if you are moving about 2,000 steps per day, try for 3,000 as a new goal. If you are doing 10,000 a day right now, try for 11,000 or to at least maintain your efforts. Typically, 10,000 steps per day translates to about four to five miles, depending on stride length. Sounds like a lot, I know, but remember this can (and should, if possible) be spread out throughout the day; it does not have to be done all at once. That is why it is important to keep an eye on your steps with your phone. Using an app will automatically track your movements (because, admit it, we all have our phones on us most of the day) and give us good information on how much we are actually moving throughout the day. Moral of the story is, if you can add steps into your day, do it.

Micro-movement life hack #3: When you are putting away your laundry, don't make stacks and then put each stack away. Fold one item, walk to where that item belongs, and put it away. Rinse. Repeat. Do this with each item you are folding. Sounds crazy, I know, but it probably will only take you only an extra three to five minutes per basket load. I understand this is three to five fewer minutes you could potentially be binge watching *Xena*, but again, it's worth the effort to add extra movement to your day. Micro interventions are where it's at, folks!

Micro-movement life hack #4: Integrate work and social life with physical activity. My co-workers know that I prefer to have walking meetings over regular office meetings, so they come prepared with tennis shoes when we are scheduled to chat. We literally take our notepads or phones, walk the halls, chat, and stop occasionally to take down notes. I find it not only supports our physical health, but also gives an extra "umph" to our meetings in terms of brainstorming. I always have better ideas when I am up and moving around or going for walks, so this can generate some great creativity in my professional life. And when I get home from work and want to socialize with my friends, I ask them to go for a hike with me. I know if I just hung out with my friends after work, we would probably end up having a cocktail and some snacks. By taking a walk with them, I can reduce caloric intake, expend more calories, and impact many different dimensions of wellness while having an amazing time catching up with friends.

Let's talk a bit more about this cardio stuff. Aside from moving more and sitting less, there are some more concrete guidelines we should all be striving to achieve. Remember, just raising your heart and breathing rate is what we are looking for here. The second guideline is to do 150 to 300 minutes of moderate intensity or 75 to 150 minutes of vigorous intensity exercise, or a combination of the two, each week. Some of you might be thinking, "Come on Carrie, you just told me I could walk to my mailbox for exercise and now you're telling me I need to get five hours of exercise a week? That is quite a leap." OK, first remember to do what you can and then slowly ratchet that up from there. If you are currently walking the dog for ten minutes a day, five days per week, that is fabulous! Can you set a goal of 15 minutes per day five days a week for next week? Or add an extra 15-minute walk to your routine a couple days a week? Take baby steps to get there; you don't have to go "all in" to achieve these guidelines all at once. And if you are already meeting those goals, please try to increase from there, too, if you can. Movement is great for all systems of your body, not just your waistline, and the more you can do, the better you will feel. Cardio work can help you manage your weight, but also helps keep your heart and lungs healthy, your digestive system working well, and your emotions and mental health in check, and prevents chronic illnesses like cardiovascular disease, diabetes, and some cancers, too. I am going to say this again. Move more, sit less. Yes, it is that important.

Micro-movement life hack #5: Exercise snacks. Here's the next little tidbit: you can break these minutes up into small little bite-sized exercise chunks if that works better for you, or what I like to call exercise snacking! Try going for a 20-minute walk in the morning and one in the evening. That is 40 minutes per day. Multiply that by seven days and you get 280 minutes per week; a sweet spot! This does not have to be overwhelming; just think up a little exercise snack and then you can fit it in when you can sometime during the day. A ten-minute workout video here, a 30-minute lawn mow there, and voila, you reach the recommendation! Here is an exercise snack life hack I employ, and you probably are all going to think I have a screw loose, but here goes. When I bought my house, the previous owner left an old-fashioned mower in the garage. Like a spinning blades, death trap for the toes kind of mower. I do not have a big yard at all, so I decided that instead of mowing my lawn with the brand-new gas-powered mower I had purchased, I would try push-mowing the old-fashioned way so that I could take better care of Mother Nature. I intentionally want to help out the environment with this intervention, but boy, am I getting a good workout, too! No wonder people had small yards in the 1950s! It's hard work! But this also counts toward my cardio minutes per week. Micro-movement interventions add up.

Strength training is the next area of movement humans need to stay healthy. Strength training does not mean you are deadlifting or bench pressing at the gym. You can do strength training with small hand weights, resistance bands, or even just your body weight. Don't believe me? Try doing a wall sit or a plank for a minute. Body weight will do just fine, thank you! Now of course if you want to gain muscle mass, not just strength, you will need to start pushing some metal around, but this is a foundational book, so we will just chat about resistance exercises.

Micro-movement life hack #6: Wall pushups. In between meetings at the office or loads of laundry at home, stop for 60 seconds, face the wall, and place your hands out in front of you on the wall. Do a pushup, five pushups, ten pushups, whatever you can do until you reach the point of "my muscles are pooped out right now" tiredness. The farther away from the wall you place your feet, the harder it is to do this. This is strength building!

Micro-movement life hack #7: Lift up your feet. You heard me right. When you are sitting down to dinner, watching a movie, or sitting at your computer, lift both feet up off the ground. It doesn't have to be far off the ground, but the farther off, the more difficult it will be, meaning the more you will be engaging your core and lower body muscles. Lift both feet off of the floor at the same time and hold. If you can, try to not hold onto your chair with your hands or arms; simply lift those feet up off of the ground using your core muscles. Hold for as long as you can and then put them back down. Repeat as often as you would like. If that is too difficult, start with just alternating raising and holding each leg, one at a time. You see, I am not asking you to spend hours in the gym each week. If you have the means, ability, and desire to do that, please do so, but my intent with these micro-movement intervention ideas is to get you thinking about how you can weave physical activity into your daily life without feeling like it is overwhelming or oppressive. Basically, things you can sneak into your day to get benefits from without devoting large chunks of time. Start small; exercise snack. This is how you gain traction and build confidence for larger future gains in our continuous quality improvements.

Now back to the guidelines. You should be doing some sort of resistance or strength training at least two days per week. You need to be hitting all of the major muscle groups. It may work better for you to do the upper body one day and the lower body another day, but you can certainly combine both on the same day, whatever you are comfortable with. You can use resistance bands or body weight exercises, or you could do things like take a Pilates or yoga class, too. Whatever focuses on building strength as opposed to focusing on raising your heart and breathing rate; that is what I am looking for here. This will help you to maintain your bone and muscle strength, help manage your weight, and decrease your risk of slips, trips, and falls as you age.

Flexibility, ugh. Yes, I know we need this! Flexibility is all too often overlooked in terms of physical well-being, but nonetheless it is super important to help prevent injuries. Joints that can move as intended simply function better, so that when you are working on the cardio or strength training, you will have less risk for injuries and less pain. Maintaining your flexibility as you age can also help you in maintaining your activities of daily living, like being able to reach up high in the cupboards or being able to turn around to look behind you while you are backing your car down the driveway. It can also help to prevent those slips, trips, and falls as we age. Plus, it just feels good and can help you relax, too! Incorporate a stretching routine for all major muscle groups a couple days per week.

Micro-movement life hack #8: Stretch for five minutes before you go to bed at night. You can use an app on your phone or just do what feels good for you. Stretching before bed can help you be more relaxed, be mindful, and support a better night's rest, which can also help your emotional dimension of wellness.

Finally, we need to talk about the last guideline, balance—something that is so often overlooked but vitally important as we age. Our balance can actually start to wane in our 30s! For those of us that have more around the middle, past injuries, or pain, balance can be a bigger challenge. You need good core muscles for good balance. How are those tummy muscles treating you these days? As we sit in front of screens longer and longer each passing year, our core muscles become weakened. Paying attention to them is important, again, to prevent those falls, trips, and slips. I know it might not seem like a big deal to someone in their 30s or 40s, but unless we are aware of this and actually practice balance activities during those decades, poor balance will sneak up on us quickly.

Micro-movement life hacks #9–11: When you are doing the dishes or standing in line at the grocery store, stand on one foot. Walk heel to toe forward and backward across the living room when you go pick up the remote. When you get up out of the chair or out of bed, don't use your hands; rely only on your core muscles to do the work. Little things like that go a long way because you are engaging your core and forcing your brain to recall stabilization efforts.

Bottom line: the more you move, the better. The less garbage you consume, the better. Here is a list of some things you can do to support your physical health.

- Walk every day, even if it is just to the mailbox and back; whatever you can do, do it
- Continuously work to increase your movement every day
- Test your well water annually
- Integrate your social connectedness with activity, like hiking or biking with friends
- Avoid sugar and the 60+ different names it uses to hide from you
- Read labels
- Measure your amount of food intake and use an app on your phone to get a better idea of how many calories you are actually taking in every day
- Brainstorm life hacks that work for you
- Become a dog walker volunteer at the Humane Society
- Use a movement or pedometer app on your phone
- Do balance exercises every day; just one or two minutes is effective
- Buy local foods; know your farmer, know your food
- Join a group fitness class
- Bike or walk to work, school, appointments, shopping, church . . . you get the idea
- Smile
- Take the stairs

Drink water, coffee, or tea that is unsweetened

Hug people

Park further away

Avoid processed foods, including artificial sweeteners

Bring real food to potlucks and social gatherings

Try a new sport

Garden

Push-mow your lawn

Stretch

Plank

Pet animals

Send real foods like watermelon or star fruit slices to school for your kids' birthday treats

Sing

Wash your hands more often

Limit alcohol

Lobby your workplace and schools to remove soda machines from the buildings

Avoid smoking, vaping, and drug use

Get routine medical checkups and dental care

Have a medical home and a consistent primary care provider

Use only one pharmacy

Use sunscreen

Know your numbers (blood pressure, blood sugar, cholesterol)

Now it's your turn! Tell me what your strengths and opportunities are in this dimension.

Strengths:

Opportunities:

Next up, I want you to write down one or two things that you realistically might be able to do in the next couple of months to support your physical dimension of wellness. Just make sure that they are realistic for you to do.

> Intervention(s):
>
> _____
>
> _____
>
> _____

So, this is Act One of your life, everyone. We have taken an inventory of what healthy looks like and doesn't look like in the three determinants and eight dimensions of wellness. You have had the challenge of writing down in black and white, or maybe using a purple pen if you are flamboyant, what your strengths and opportunities are in each of the dimensions based on your life up until this point. It is my hope that you have been able to identify the interconnectedness of the determinants and the dimensions without me shining the stage light on them.

What now? First things first. I want you to rewrite your definition of health and wellness. Hopefully it has changed since the first writing. I will also share my personal definition with you. Everyone has their own definition based on their values, beliefs, lived experiences, current status, goals, and aspirations. It changes. Or at least it should, because we all learn as we live; we are all continuous quality improvement projects. Unless you are enlightened, you should never stop growing, changing, and learning, and that takes continuous effort. In the Act Two, I will Sherpa you through taking these baselines measures and ideas and turning them into new growth. Hold tight. Let's start first with a few takeaways from this chapter, though.

Recall your top five values. Write them down here:

List your biggest "aha" moments from the content you learned in Act One:

List your biggest personal takeaways from Act One; think about your own lived experiences and life stories, and how these have shaped your current state of health and well-being:

Reflect on your takeaways and your values that you listed above. Now tell me what your personal definition of health and wellness is, in your own words, as it is important to you, right here, right now. Three to five sentences. There is no right or wrong way here; just go with your gut. This is all about you:

Now write down what is different between your first definition and your current definition:

As promised, I will share my own definition of health and wellness.

"Health is a constant interplay of multidimensional actions and inactions that serve to seek balance in my life. Wellness is an active awareness and coordination of my internal motivations to maximize my strengths and minimize my opportunities."

As you can see, I broke my definitions up between health and wellness, acknowledging that though they are intrinsically dependent upon one another, it is just easier for my brain to delineate the two. This definition aligns with my values and beliefs and is broad enough to help guide my decision making in all dimensions. This is my Sherpa in my health and wellness journey. This is just my definition. There are hundreds of definitions out there that one can pick from, but personally speaking, I think it is far more meaningful to create your own than to use what someone else has created. Once you are happy with your personal definition, write it down and put it somewhere you will see it every day: the bathroom mirror, refrigerator, office computer, whatever works for you. This will be your gentle reminder to guide daily life choices.

After reviewing all of your aha's and takeaways from Act One, but before we move on to Act Two, I need you to answer a few items. This will help guide our upcoming work on transformative and sustainable behavior change.

Questions

#1: What are the top two things you love or really like about yourself and/or your life?

_____

_____

These are your strengths.

#2: What are two areas that you think you could improve upon that are important to you right now?

_____

_____

These are your opportunities for growth.

#3: Of those two things, what is the low-hanging fruit that you could pick first to work on (if and when you so choose)?

_____

_____

You can use this to create your first goal in the coming chapter.

#4: And how ready or able are you to address the lowest of the hanging fruit right now? Rank this on a scale of 1 to 4, with 1 being Harry Potter dealing with Uncle Vernon in the first movie and 4 being Harry Potter fighting Voldemort in the last movie kind of ready.

1 2 3 4

This is your level of readiness to change.

No judgment here! If you are not ready, you are not ready, and that is perfectly fine. We all have our own timeline. I can help facilitate your change to better prepare you for the getting ready step, or to get ready for the actual changes themselves in the next chapter.

The show must go on!

Onward to Act Two! Take an intermission break here though; that was a ton of content we went through in this chapter. Go for a walk, rest and relax, meditate, play with your kids, do some laundry, maybe even have a glass of wine in one of those little sippy cups they give you at the theatre, and just think about all of this stuff we covered. You are not cramming for a big test; digestion time is good when you are working toward a healthier you.

CHAPTER SEVEN

ACT TWO

Welcome back to the show! I hope you had a lovely intermission and enjoyed the sippy cup of wine. So far, we have spent the majority of this book analyzing your past character development to help you become aware of all the components that comprise your Act One. In the next step, we will talk about how you can successfully transition into Act Two by identifying the props and script you need to make this a smashing hit. That's right, we are going to explore what I mean by all of that "sustainable behavior change" stuff I have been rambling on about in the first six chapters. By really taking a hard look at your sum parts in those first six chapters (all those little love notes I had you write to yourself along the way), we can better understand all of the components that have brought you to your current state of wellness. This chapter will use a couple of different theoretical behavior change models to explain "the why behind the what" and to (hopefully) evoke behavior change or at least explain how behavior change happens, so that when you are ready to make changes you can tackle them head on with the knowledge of how to make your chosen interventions stick.

Before we jump into the different models and theories of behavior change, I want you to envision an art gallery in the halls of our theatre. This is a great place to go whenever you might need an intermission break as we work through some of this stuff, because this leg of the journey might give you some feelings. In this hallway gallery, imagine there are hundreds of pieces of artwork, all beautifully framed. Each of these paintings represents an emotion and mind state that you have experienced or may experience at some time in your life. Different abstractions, shades, and intensity levels of happiness, excitement, anxiety, sadness, worry, elation, irritability, every emotion possible. In your mind's eye, what do these emotions look like in the paintings? Envision them while you name them. Make these emotions come to life in your mind's eye. Then frame them. The frames are the mechanisms of mindfulness, putting those emotions into perspective instead of letting them roll over the top of you and consume you. Recall that the skill of being mindful includes the ability to be aware, to be in the present moment, and to allow what's happening to happen without judgment, clinging, or pushing away. The viewing of these emotions in mindfulness frames is a way for us to appreciate that these are just emotions that will come and go. The emotions will pass as we journey down the hallway and look at the next piece of art, and the next, and so on. Just as we move onward viewing the different pieces of art on our walk down the hallway, so too do our emotions change and move onward. Framing the paintings with mindfulness helps us to contain, then label and finally accept the emotions, and hence supports our capacity to respond instead of react to the emotions. It offers us control and comfort, especially when the emotions are difficult to corral and feel bigger than ourselves in the moment. Emotions like sadness or anxiety can be powerful and can derail our efforts to change behavior by getting you "stuck" looking at that one picture in the hallway for too long. This process of viewing the emotions without lingering on any one piece allows us the ability to appreciate the artful properties of emotion, then move to the next painting in the gallery, appreciating each for what it offers you at any given moment throughout your different stages of life, and each can give you the wisdom of lived experiences. Everything is in a constant state of change. Your mindset will be too when attempting behavior change. You will more than likely hold excitement and eagerness when thinking about a new behavior change, daydreaming about the potential that this change may bring to your life. But as the weeks roll on, you may grow bored or overwhelmed trying to secure that sustainability piece of change. To secure this change, you need to be mindful of not only your actions that move you toward that goal, but your mind state, and labeling and being aware of your emotions. This theatre gallery analogy is a way for you to more easily identify and verbalize what you are feeling and then to let it go.

Now that we are aware of the importance of our mind state and emotions and how to take a step back from letting those emotions derail us, let's jump into behavior change models and theories. I know, I know, it does not sound exciting, but I will ask you to trust me one more time. It's exciting stuff; this stuff actually kind of geeks me out a bit (is that TMI?).

Here is a very brief introduction of what behavior change theory is to begin with. A theory is basically a summation of ideas that some folks agree upon to explain something or make connections to phenomena. A model is very similar, but is more of a representation built off of a theory that is used to explain or predict something. There are a zillion theories and models out there (OK, maybe not a zillion, but a lot) and you can find theories that are unique to every profession. I am going to focus on just a few of them that are specific to actual behavior change since this is part of the script you will need to embrace wellness in your life.

We have already explored a model in the fourth chapter—the ecological model—where we can look at health from an individual level all the way to a societal level to help us explain current and past health status and lifestyle choices, and predict future health outcomes. In this chapter, we are going to focus more on an individual level: what happens when you personally embark on a wellness change. Knowing this information can help support your work so that you can identify where you are at in the behavior change process and then tailor which interventions would best work for you at that given moment. Think about this chapter as your super special decoder ring. With this information, you can help figure out your "why behind the what," as I like to call it—why you are driven to make (or not make) certain health-related changes.

The first model we will look at is pretty standard for behavior change professionals. It is called the Transtheoretical Model of Change. From now on we will just call this the TTM, because that is a mouthful. There is no quiz at the end of this chapter, so don't get hung up on the vocabulary, just process the information and try to think of an example in your own life as we talk about these models to make them more understandable and applicable directly to you. I will also offer lots of examples along the way to better articulate what these mean and look like in real life.

OK! Here we go! The TTM had five stages of behavior change to it originally, and then it was modified to include six. I'll explain. These stages are precontemplation, contemplation, preparation, action, maintenance, and termination. Let's chat about each of these and then review a couple examples to help make this make sense.

The precontemplation stage means that you have no desire to make any sort of behavior change. Now this could be because you think your behaviors are just fine, like, "I'm doing great, nothing to see here, keep 'er moving." Or it may be because you have tried to change so many times that you think it is completely unattainable, so "why even bother?" Or the thought of any type of behavior change may just be too overwhelming to even ponder, so you set your mind to the other 87 things on your to-do list for the day. It's easier to just ignore it at this point. As you can see, there is no behavior change happening in this stage.

Next is contemplation. You may start to think, "Well, it might be good if I change XYZ in my life at some point." You might start to think that your behavior may have some negative consequences to it, or you may get this tickle in the back of your mind that says, "Yeah, I know I have tried and failed a million times, but I think I might need to try to change again because XYZ is kind of bothering me." So basically you are toying with the idea that at some point you might make a change because it could potentially benefit you, but you are just not ready to commit to the idea of change yet. You can see the potential benefits, but it is more comfortable to stay where you are right now.

Then we get to the preparation stage. At this stage you are thinking along the lines of, "OK, I know I need to change this, I'm going to get a game plan together." At this point in the model the person is committed to change, as opposed to maintaining the status quo, and will take some baby steps to lay the foundation and get ready for the actual change. In the preparation stage the scales have been tipped to weigh more heavily in the "I need to change" camp than the "I am comfortable remaining in my current state" camp.

Here's the magic: action! stage. Yup, you guessed it. You are actually making the behavior change now. In this stage of the model, you are committed to the change because you can see there are more pros than cons to change, you have prepared both mentally and physically for the change, and you take the leap to change. You may slip, trip, stumble, or fumble, but you are doing it just like you planned out in the preparation stage, or you have made tweaks to the goal based on life circumstances, but you're still making forward progress. Either way, you plan on keeping the change going.

The maintenance stage is where you have made forward progress during the action stage, and it actually stuck. This usually takes root after several months of consistent action-stage behavior. The pros continue to outweigh any cons you have experienced during the change and the change is becoming a habit, and not requiring too much thought to continue the desired behavior. The goal of this stage is to prevent relapsing and to, you got it, maintain the behavior change.

Termination was added a bit later after the initial creation of this model. Termination means that there is absolutely no way the individual will revert back to the old behavior. There is no thought to the behavior anymore, it is just what life has become. Honestly, I am a little on the fence with this one. I think in some circumstances and with certain behaviors you can achieve this, but maybe not with others. Let me give you some examples from each side of the so-called fence. I actually used to be a smoker a long time ago. I never thought I could achieve the termination stage. I cycled through all of these other stages so many times, even the maintenance stage, and still went back to smoking again and again. But I can comfortably say that I am in the termination phase now. It has been over 20 years since my last cigarette and quite frankly, it makes me sick when I smell someone else doing it, and when I am stressed, I never think of reaching for a smoke, so I know for a fact that I will never ever go back to it. Voila! The termination stage. Some folks, on the other hand, may be in that maintenance phase for the rest of their life when struggling with addictions. It can be a daily challenge to actively say no on a regular basis. So that is why I am on the fence with this one. It really is highly dependent on the individual and based on the level of difficulty in eliminating the behavior. Quitting a diet cola habit is one thing. Quitting highly addictive substances like alcohol or drugs or stopping highly addictive behaviors like gambling is a whole different ballpark. I don't want to undermine or undervalue the daily effort it takes to avoid these substances or behaviors, sometimes for a lifetime.

So there is the model. Please keep in mind that people do not progress through each stage in a linear, sequential fashion. A person may go from contemplation to action in a day (for all of us hair-trigger decision makers out there!). A person may be stuck in precontemplation their entire lives in regard to a certain health behavior, simply happy with or unaware of where they are in their current state of (un)wellness. A person can be in the maintenance phase for two years and then slide back into their old behaviors in the snap of a finger (or the flick of a lighter at your best friend's wedding in Vegas). We are all unique and at different stages for different behavior changes at any given moment. But here is the thing. If you are thinking about a behavior change, and I am assuming you are since you are reading this book, then it is helpful to know about this model, identify where you are to help you better prepare for that change, and embrace certain interventions at certain times, so in turn you can be more likely to achieve sustainable change, meaning change that gets you into that maintenance or even termination phase. With your super special decoder ring, you can better mitigate barriers and pave the road for success. Let's work on a high-level overview example so you can make more sense of this.

Precontemplation: I am very happy treating myself with my diet cola every morning. It wakes me up, I get fluids, I am taking in no calories or sugar, and I feel just fine. Don't even try to tell me this is a bad thing. It makes me happy and when I am happy everyone else around me is happy, too. My employees are very thankful that I start my day with a diet cola, and you should be too, so just stop talking to me about this.

Contemplation: Well, my dentist just told me that my enamel is wearing thin and that it is probably because of this diet cola habit I have. She said that if I don't curb that, some not-so-great things are going to happen to these chompers. Did I mention I really do not care for going to the dentist? It freaks me out, actually. So thinking about spending more time in that chair outside of my regular cleaning appointments is kinda too much for my brain cells to accept. Not going to lie. Maybe it's time I start to think about this diet cola thing.

Preparation: So after my little chitchat with Dr. Dentist, I started to research what happens to my body when I drink diet cola. Turns out it not only ruins my teeth but other bones in my body too, and it actually makes me hungrier than I would be without it. I am just going to put it out there, I don't want to add any more pounds than I have to. I need to be able to play hide-and-seek with my grandkids on the weekends, and if I didn't have my real chompers, I think I would feel embarrassed and uncomfortable in social settings. I am starting to figure out what I like or at least what I can tolerate as a substitute for the miraculous diet cola at 0600 every day. I started asking my friends what they drink in the morning. I bought some small packages of different coffees and different black teas to sample to see which ones I might like. I'm going to try a different one each day this week, but I am still going to have my diet cola too, because I am not quite ready to give that up just yet. I know I need to, and I will, I just have to get all of my ducks in a row before I take the deep dive.

Action: I did it! I might not be too happy about leaving my diet cola behind me, but I decided that this black tea thing isn't so bad, and I actually like it. It gives me a bit of a kick in the morning, I am not adding sugar or milk to it, so it is calorie free, and it is not hurting my teeth. I get my electric hot water kettle, my mug, and the tea bag all ready in the evening before I go to bed, so that all I have to do is stumble to the kettle and flip the switch in the morning. Easy peasy. Sometimes I brew a pitcher of the stuff and just keep it in the refrigerator so I can have a glass of iced tea right away without even having to wait for the kettle to warm up. People around me don't seem to notice, or at least they don't tell me I am grumpy in the morning without it.

Maintenance: Well, I left behind the diet cola for about six months now and I feel pretty good. I just had my regular cleaning with my dentist, and she said my teeth look better already. I am not feeling so hungry all the time anymore, so I am actually eating less during the day, too. I think I can stick this out. I like how I feel. I actually crave tea more often than I think about soda, and even when I go to a restaurant, I order iced tea instead of a diet cola, so I am not even "treating" myself with one every now and then like I did when I first made the switch.

Termination: It's been years since I drank that last diet cola. I really don't even think about it anymore, but when I see someone drinking one, I think to myself, "Man, I am happy I kicked that habit and still have all of my chompers secured safely in my head."

Now that you have a better idea of what the stages actually look like in action, here are the interventions that you can use in each of these stages to help you progress on to the next stage and hopefully onward to sustainable behavior change. I'll use an example once more to help give you a better idea of what these interventions can "look like" to move you from one stage to the next, and so that you can better apply this model to your own life.

> Precontemplation: Honestly, there is not much we can do here in terms of interventions to move you to contemplation. If you have zero desire to change, change is not going to happen. But one intervention to help progress on to the next stage would be simply keeping an open mind to information that others might be sharing with you. Let's use conserving water for this example. You may be thinking, "There are tons of rivers and lakes all around me. Why on earth would I need to limit how much water I use? I pay for it; I will use it when I want. No one is going to tell me how many minutes I can or can't be in the shower—get out of my bathroom, Big Brother!" Information that could be coming toward you about this topic may be your teenager talking to you about water conservation efforts and how she values that for herself and future generations, or the increasing costs of water in your community, or news articles talking about drought conditions lowering reservoir levels in adjacent counties. You might hear and see this information but not really care or think about it too much. The intervention to be able to progress from this stage to the next would be to just keep an open mind to the information that is coming in front of you.
>
> Contemplation: So you've had enough "looks" from your teenager when you let the sprinklers run while it was raining and the last water bill just came and it made you clench up a wee bit when you opened it. You start to think about the pros

and cons of maybe curbing your water habit. The intervention to move you to the next stage when you are in the contemplation stage is the decisional balance that we talked about earlier. Do you think the pros outweigh the cons of this change? Does getting rid of the angsty teen looks and decreasing your water bill sound like more of a positive than continuing with the sprinkler habit? If the answer is yes, then you will more than likely move on to the next stage, which is preparation.

Preparation, as you will recall, means just that. You are preparing for the change. In this stage you might actually have a conversation with your teenager about what she learned in her science class about conservation efforts; you might start reading articles about drought conditions and how they impact everyone, not just those that are in the drought-stricken community, and you may start researching alternative ways of watering your garden, like using a rain barrel, and how much it costs to purchase one compared to the current and future water rates. You are creating a plan for change, thinking about things like where you can buy a rain barrel from, where you would set it up in your yard, and determining the right size to meet your needs. To move on to the action stage, you need to have a realistic plan in place, feel comfortable with that plan, and have not only the external factors we have been talking about, but also have the internal motivation to embrace the change. You have to feel like this water conservation is actually doable and easy to manage, and actually believe you can do it. When those come together, you can move onward to the action stage.

As you move into the action stage, you are actually doing it! You will probably feel excitement about bringing your plan to fruition. You might falter a bit as you encounter barriers that you might not have thought of, but you figure out workarounds for those. You purchase the rain barrel and set it up in your yard. You are using the water from the barrel to water your garden and flowers. But maybe the rain barrel is now breeding mosquitos and your neighbors are grumpy with you about that. Or maybe you are grumpy that you can't take three showers a day just to warm up, because you live in frozen tundra and don't know what warmth is for six months at a crack. You might even revert back to one of the first three stages if you just can't overcome these barriers to sustain the behavior change. But here is the thing. To move onward to the next stage, which is ultimately what we are all working on—that sustainable piece of behavior change—then we need to find routine, create a habit of the new behavior through consistency, and appreciate that the positives of the change continue to outweigh the negatives, which will help you continue to have that decisional balance to stay in the pro category rather than the con category. That is how you transition to the maintenance stage.

Maintenance is what we are seeking when we try to change our behaviors, that sustainability piece. This comes with changing our mindset to the point where you have been doing the change for a significant amount of time, it has become a habit, and you are happy about that habit; it feels good. So instead of being grumpy that you can't take three showers a day to stay warm, you find a workaround and just hunker down under a heated blanket when you get chilled, or you keep the rain barrel as a contained unit with a cover so mosquitoes don't find their way in and breed in it. These things make the behavior change fit into your life with little thought or effort. The intervention to make this change stick forever, meaning you get to the termination phase, is to simply stop thinking about it. Easier than it sounds!

In the termination phase, you got it: the behavior is just what's "normal" for you, meaning you do not think about it at all. You forget that sprinkling was even a thing. You are super happy with your water bill, and you can get shamed by your teenager for other things, like wearing flip-flops with socks out in public.

So there you have it, folks, the **TTM**. Not so overwhelming, right? Now it's your turn. I want you to think about a health behavior change that you have made in the past and break it down into the different stages like I did. You may have cycled through the different stages several times or may not have achieved all of the stages yet; no worries, this is all about you and what you want to think about right now.

Behavior change topic:

_____

Precontemplation:

_____

Contemplation:

_____

Preparation:

Action:

Maintenance:

Termination:

Excellent work, my friends! The next model we are going to talk about is another very common tool for health professionals, called the Health Belief Model, or the HBM. There are seven parts to this one, but it's still manageable, no worries. I promise, the next and final one we will talk about has the fewest number of moving parts to it!

The HBM focuses more on a person's beliefs, values, and attitudes to help better understand behavior change success. Do those sound familiar at all? I sure hope so! Keep those and this model in mind—we will be taking a deep dive into them in the next chapter!

The parts of the HBM include perceived susceptibility, perceived benefits, perceived barriers, perceived seriousness, modifying variables, cues to action, and self-efficacy. Again, no need to memorize these; we will chat about each one and I will give you an example to better explain just like I did with the last one. But first, a quick definition of each one.

> Perceived susceptibility: This is how likely it is you think you will get a disease or have a negative outcome from a behavior.
>
> Perceived benefits: These are your thoughts on if the new behavior will reap more benefits than what you are currently doing.
>
> Perceived barriers: These are your thoughts on what might prevent you from adopting the new behavior.
>
> Perceived seriousness: This is your thought on how terrible it will be if you get a disease or how terrible the negative consequence of the behavior would be.
>
> Modifying variables: These are your own unique personal life factors that will affect whether or not you make the behavior change.
>
> Cues to action: These things encourage you to begin the change.
>
> Self-efficacy: This is your belief in yourself and your ability to actually make the change. It is probably the most important factor right here. Think of the Little Engine That Could. If you think you can, you are far more likely to change than the Debbie Downer that has no belief in herself or her ability to change.

Now that you know about these different moving parts and what they mean, I will walk you through an example. I will use my own personal drive for candy as an example of this.

Setting the stage: I love candy. Not like gummy bears and Sweet Tarts kind of candy, but that lovely, ooey, gooey, chocolatey, nutty, caramely kind of candy. I really don't care for ice cream, but when people go get ice cream, I'm ready to rock and roll right there with them because I know I can just buy the most egregious kind of ice cream just so that I can pick out all of the candy bits. The ice cream is just the vehicle to get those chunks of goodness into my mouth. Can you tell how much I love candy? Well, I also told you already about my genetic predisposition for diabetes, and these two things don't mix all that well together. Here we go with my candy problem and use of the HBM to explain and/or predict my candy-seeking behaviors.

> Perceived *susceptibility*: I know that I am already predisposed to acquiring diabetes. My grandma and uncle both have diabetes, and my genetic report confirmed my predisposition. This, in addition to my candy habit, is working against me. I know I am *susceptible* to illness, which gives me pause.
>
> Perceived *benefits*: I know that if I limit my ooey-gooey goodness intake, it will lessen the likelihood of acquiring the disease. I also know that if I reduce my sugar intake, my blood sugar levels will more than likely continue to remain within the normal limits, I will feel better, I won't be as hungry, and I will have a lesser likelihood of a whole host of other problems that come with sugar use that we already talked about in Chapter Six. Therefore, my *perceived benefits* are stabilized

blood sugar, feeling better physically, and decreased hunger if I curb my sugar habit.

Perceived *barriers*: I live within walking distance of an ice cream shop with huge chunks of candy integrated into all of their ice creams (in mammoth portion sizes). When I am tired or upset or after a big meal, my sweet tooth rages and I have a poor locus of control to prevent candy binging at that time. My *perceived barriers* to limiting my sugar consumption are the proximity of the ice cream shop and my raging sweet tooth issues.

Perceived *seriousness*: As a nurse, I know how serious diabetes is. At best, I will have to take a pill every day. If it gets worse, a shot every day, and if it gets even worse, I'll start to lose toes and limbs. This is nothing to joke about. My *perceived seriousness* is that this disease is bad news and can impact my current and future health poorly.

Modifying variables: I have personal past experience of eating too much candy. I don't like the way I feel afterward; my stomach is no bueno and I gain weight. I don't like that. That motivates me to not have candy-seeking behaviors. Intellectually speaking, I also know better, as I have seen firsthand what diabetes can do to a person. I am a nurse, so my education influences my choices. I am financially stable and the ice cream store is close to where I live, so I can walk down to the ice cream shop and order that large hunk of goodness if I want to. My culture and societal norms say it is perfectly normal to order ice cream as big as my head and eat it all too; this is a treat that I can indulge in whenever I want to. I can get my furry friends a doggie cone while I am there, and I know they love that, too. (See, there are good and bad variables here, sending my brain conflicting messages.) Therefore, my *modifying variables* are being able to afford the candy, knowing candy gorging is socially acceptable with both friends and furry friends, understanding that I might feel sick after eating so much, and that my sweet tooth can be ramped up based off of my emotions.

Cues to action: The things that could prevent me from getting that candy-laden ice cream could be me stepping on the scale this morning and seeing a scary number, noticing my sugar cravings are getting out of control (positive feedback loop issues), seeing a sibling or parent get diagnosed with diabetes, seeing healthy, sugar-free recipes on my social media feed, and meal planning sugar-free meals for the week with my kiddo (you see the cues to action can go both ways here, too, sending my brain conflicting messages). My cues to action can include stepping on my scale, planning for and buying sweet alternatives, and being mindful of my physical and emotional cravings.

Self-efficacy: "I think I can, I think I can!" with gusto! And I actually believe in myself that I can resist the candy craving. On a scale of 1 to 4, with 1 being "No way no how Scooby wants to go into the haunted house," to 4 being "Heck yeah, I'll take that Scooby snack!", I am going to give myself a solid 3 for this one. Most days I am good at avoiding sweets, but there are times when I am overtired and stressed when I might falter. My *self-efficacy* means I feel pretty good about my ability to make this change.

So this model really is about weights and balances. Do the pros outweigh the cons? If so, then positive behavior change will be more likely. Add in a healthy dose of self-efficacy, and you have a winning combination for sustainable behavior change. In my example, the pros outweigh the cons, and I am pretty sure of myself that I can maintain this candy-avoidant behavior. I identified what my barriers to behavior change are and I try my best to avoid those. Most days I am not tempted, and this is pretty sustainable for me. Instead of a regular field trip to the ice cream shop, that is left for only super special occasions, and I can order the baby serving size, so it's only about as big as my dog's head instead of mine.

Now it is your turn. I want you to think about a behavior change *that you have not made yet*, one that you are just toying with for right now, and apply these moving parts to that potential change. You may want to review your notes in the dimensions of wellness area in Chapter Five to review your identified areas of opportunity if you can't think of a concrete change you might want to embark upon now or in the future.

Future behavior change idea:

_____

_____

Perceived susceptibility:

_____

_____

Perceived benefits:

Perceived barriers:

Perceived seriousness:

Modifying variables:

Cues to action:

On a scale of 1 to 4, with 1 being "No way no how Scooby wants to go into the haunted house," to 4 being "Heck yeah, I'll take that Scooby snack!", how confident are you in yourself to make this change?

> Self-efficacy:
>
> 1   2   3   4

Now, I would like you to think about this future behavior change example that you used for the HBM and reflect on what that means in terms of the TTM. Remember that precontemplation means there is no interest or seemingly no ability to make the change. Contemplation means that you are toying with the idea of change, but the cons outweigh the pros at this point. Preparation means that the scales have tipped, the pros outweigh the cons, and you are getting ready to make the change. Circle what stage you think you are in right now for this anticipated change.

> Precontemplation
>
> Contemplation
>
> Preparation

OK, last one! This one is my favorite because this is how I kicked my panic attacks in the butt. This, in combination with the information that we have already gone through, worked for me. I hope it can work for your sustainable behavior change desires, too. The final tool to help explain behavior change is called the Self-Efficacy Theory. Yes, we did just talk about self-efficacy as a part of the HBM, so you are already familiar with what self-efficacy is, but if you took a break between there and here, I will remind you. It is the belief in yourself that you can actually do what you are setting out to do.

I think you can kind of see by now that the main content of this book is to get you in the right headspace. Change won't happen in any dimension of wellness until your mind allows it to happen and supports your efforts in a continuous fashion. You see there are two different types of motivating factors (what drives us to change): intrinsic and extrinsic. Intrinsic comes from within you. Extrinsic comes from outside of you. Extrinsic factors are those that you can't control: the weather (not going for a walk because it's raining), social pressure (my friend had the second piece of cheesecake so that means it is totally acceptable for me to do that, too), community and societal norms (my city offers a different 5K every weekend; we are a running community, it's just what we do here), and cultural influences (I was raised to respect women and therefore would never consider raising my voice or hand to my mom, sisters, or partner). While extrinsic factors influence behaviors both negatively and positively, as you can see from my examples, intrinsic factors hold more weight. This is the million-dollar question right here, folks. What motivates you to change? What is your "why"? Are you wanting to change for personal betterment, for health, for longer life, for better looks, to gain intelligence, to be less of a jerk to yourself or others? These intrinsic motivating factors are all you; what is floating around in that headspace of yours. When the going gets tough, like moving from the preparation to the action stage, or the action to the maintenance stage, or when you simply just feel beat down and worn out, what will keep you going? What is the deep internal drive that will help you pick yourself back up, dust off, and get back on that stage? That is your "why" or your intrinsic motivator. You may have one or many. But it is important to keep this/these in mind with any type of behavior change. Life will kick you down. This "why" will be your path to digging deep and getting back up. In terms of trying to tackle my problem with panic attacks, which were triggered by driving on the interstate, my "whys" were the following: independence (regaining the freedom to move about without needing anyone else to do that for me), having the ability to get my kids to a hospital quickly if they ever needed it, to not ever be stranded somewhere, incapacitated to help myself, and to heal my mental health. I think you can see that these are not superficial "whys," or at least they weren't to me. They were deeply important to me. These "whys" were my intrinsic motivators to change that I had to keep in mind when the going got tough. And believe me, it was tough.

Before we head into the final theory, I want you to take a moment and list your "whys" right here. Having your "whys" clearly articulated and at the ready increases your self-efficacy and your chances for sustainable behavior change. Think back to the change that you wanted to make that you used for the HBM exercise. What change are you toying with in your mind's eye? Brainstorm your intrinsic motivators, your "whys," and write them down here:

Why(s):

_____

_____

I know I am asking you to do some hard work. You might need to think of that hallway of paintings again and take an intermission right now. If this is bringing up some scary thoughts, feelings, ideas, memories, or anxieties, take a break for a while, and on that break think about what those emotions look like in your gallery. Name your emotions. Frame those emotions in your mindfulness skill set and just sit with them for a while. Don't push them away or hit them head-on like a Chuck Norris roundhouse kick. Just stand in that theatre hallway, take an intermission break, breathe, and gander at those emotions for a spell. As you ponder, try to sit with those big feelings; watch them ebb and flow. They are just emotions that have a beginning and an end; they change just like the tide rolls in and out, just like the rustle of wind moves each leaf in a different cadence and tempo, just like the rain coming down from a heavy cloud will lighten and eventually stop. Then move on down the hallway when you're ready to.

The Self-Efficacy Theory has only four parts to it; see, I told you this one had fewer things to think about! Those four parts are mastery experience, vicarious experience, verbal persuasion, and finally, your physical and emotional states. I find that the first two models we talked about in this chapter help me with positive behavior changes, like "I should really move more" or "I should really eat real food instead of processed food" kind of changes. The Self-Efficacy Theory seems to fit me better when I need to tackle something scary or anxiety-producing. It sort of calms my headspace and gives me the courage to just be with that anxiety instead of fleeing from it or trying to pummel it over the head with the stage props. With this theory, if I believe I can accomplish the behavior change, then I am far more likely to do so. So here we are back at square one: getting into our heads again.

> Mastery experience: This means that we recall a time when we have already accomplished this behavior or action, or something similar to it.
>
> Vicarious experience: This occurs when we learn by watching someone else successfully complete the behavior or action.
>
> Verbal persuasion: This is exactly what it sounds like: someone is encouraging you through their words to accomplish the action. These are your unicorns helping you pick yourself up, dusting you off, and cheerleading for you.
>
> Physical and emotional states: This is what happens in your body and your mind when you think about or actually do the intended action.

Sounds pretty simple, right? In theory, it is! It can be difficult putting it into action, though. For this, I will use my panic attack scenario one more time to better explain what this looks like in action.

> Mastery experience: Before I started getting panic attacks, I actually loved to drive on the interstate. I found it exhilarating

and exciting. I had zero problems zipping in between cars and semis to get where I needed to go. I needed to recall these memories of success and the feelings associated with the action of driving on the interstate.

Vicarious experience: My friends all drive without issues; in fact, they had to drive me around when I was completely incapacitated from doing this. One of my friends actually drove me three hours one way to stay with a different friend who was very ill. I physically couldn't do it myself. I felt horrible because I really wanted to be with my ill friend to help her out, but I physically could not get in my car and drive myself. I love my unicorns. So I could see that all of my friends were driving on the interstate without ending up in a ball of wrecked metal and flames. Everyone else on the planet (so it seems) was able to drive on the interstate without issue. I needed to keep reminding myself of this.

Verbal persuasion: This seems like a no-brainer, but the difficulty here was I did not like to talk about my dirty little secret of being scared to death about driving on the interstate. It was embarrassing. And literally just talking about it made me break into a sweat and my heart would start to race. But if I didn't talk about it with anyone, then no one would cheer for me to give me the encouragement that I needed to do this without crashing and burning. Once I started sharing my vulnerabilities with my unicorns, then I started to get this verbal persuasion part of the equation.

Physical and emotional states: As I already shared, even when I thought about driving on the interstate, I started to panic. If I tried to get on the interstate, toying with the idea of taking the on ramp, it was a full-blown "I'm going to die and take everyone out with me" kind of moment. Cold sweat, heart racing, goofy feeling in the head like I would completely pass out in that moment. Or throw up. Or both at the same time. As I avoided the behavior more and more, the symptoms worsened. I was a mess. So here is what I did. I started meditating. As I meditated, I would imagine driving on the interstate. In great detail. What was I wearing, how did my seat belt fit, what music was playing, what time of day was it? You get the idea. Super descriptive. And I would let those feelings of anxiety come, and I would sit with them. Acknowledge them. Name them. Use mindfulness to not only frame them, but eventually tame them. And you know what? The emotions passed. Just like the clouds, the wind, the tide. They moved on, just like moving on from that framed art on the wall and getting to the next piece of artwork in my hallway. I did this exercise over and over again in the safety of my home.

As I learned how to deal with the anxiety in this safe space, I then started to stretch my wings. You see, as my panic attacks worsened and my world got smaller, I also created an issue with driving over bridges. Bridges were bad, but they were not as horrible as interstates, so I continued my journey to tackle this panic problem by driving over those. And as I would drive over the bridges, I would recall that I had driven on them in the past with success (mastery experience). No accidental lurching to the side, launching myself over the side into the abyss . . . no sirree, Bob! I would think about how thousands of people drive every day over these bridges and no harm comes to them (vicarious experience). And I would think about how my friends would cheerlead for me. And I would even cheerlead for myself out loud in the car (verbal persuasion). I am certain folks driving next to me thought I was one hand short of a stage crew, but it didn't matter; I was accepting my fear so that I could eventually get comfortable with it. I would recall the feelings of anxiety rising and falling during my mediation and remind myself that just like everything else in life, emotions are constantly changing, and that this too would pass. I felt my feet on the floor and my hands on the steering wheel. I felt the sweat dripping down my back, and I stayed with the experience without pushing it away or clinging (these are the physical and emotional states), and with time I started to get more comfortable with driving over bridges.

Once I was OK with bridges, then the next step came to driving on the interstate. Just one on ramp to the next exit at a time. And then two exits worth, and then three. Now, I am not going to sugarcoat this. It took a long time. It was horrible at times. Physically and emotionally horrible. But with time and practice, it got easier because I was able to sit with the fear, acknowledge it, name it, frame it, and eventually tame it. It's sort of like at the end of *Moana* when she is walking toward Te Fiti to restore her heart. Te Fiti is this angry, fiery goddess that is larger than life compared to Moana. But instead of battling Te Fiti or running away from her, Moana looks right up at Te Fiti with caution, grace, and bravery, and finds their common humanity. They are both hurting. In that space, they bring their foreheads together in a mutual agreement of self-compassion, and a new era of gentility and acceptance between the two is born. It becomes this beautiful evolution to bear witness to. Remember when I said that my panic attacks were actually a gift? This is what I meant. I don't know that I will ever love driving like I used to. But I no longer have to ask anyone to drive for me. I am free to go wherever I want, whenever I want. If my kids need me, I can be there in the shortest amount of time possible. And I have been able to take my meditation practice that I used to calm my driving fears and apply that to so many other aspects of my life; the gift that truly keeps on giving.

So all in all, I used the Transtheoretical Model of Change to help me prepare for the change and to know when and how to jump into action. I used the Health Belief Model to help me identify the weights and balances of the behavior change, and I used the Self-Efficacy Theory to physically and emotionally walk myself through each step of the change. Using theories or models to support behavior change help us to problem solve, to identify and try to avoid barriers, and to support intrinsic motivations for change. Decoder rings, baby! That's what I'm talking about!

Let me offer you one more example of the Self-Efficacy Theory in action. Just because I feel like it works well for conquering fears and anxieties doesn't mean that that is the be all and end all for this theory. You can use it for any ordinary behavior change you might be interested in, too. In this example we will look at the desire to be more mindful during mealtime (especially when munching down on those amazing burgers with the special sauce, and ice cream as big as your head). Here we go, a Self-Efficacy Theory example:

> *Mastery experience*: After reading the mindfulness chapter of this book, I actually took my time at work to be mindful of eating my lunch one day. I put an out-of-office response on my email for a full 30 minutes so no one would bother me. I took my packed lunch outside and sat at a picnic table. I actually tasted the sweetness of the tomatoes on my turkey sandwich, felt the sunshine on my face, and listened to the squirrels chattering while playing tag with each other. It was a lovely, peaceful experience.
>
> *Vicarious experience*: I noticed that when I go over to my friend's house for dinner, they have a screen-free zone at meal

time and actually talk to each other about their day while enjoying their meal together. They seem pretty tuned into the meal and together time. Also, I noticed that there was another person at a different picnic table doing the same thing I was doing that day at work, too. I noticed her because she didn't have her phone out; she was just watching the squirrel gymnastics show, too. I didn't know other people at work actually used those picnic tables!

Verbal persuasion: I have been working with a health coach and she has been encouraging me to unplug during mealtimes so that I can be more aware of what I am actually eating and to slow down my eating. We worked together to brainstorm ideas on why this would be a good intervention for me, and she offered words of encouragement that I could do it based on the experience I had taking my lunch outside to eat at work, and also my interest in the endeavor. I shared this information with my friend, and she said it sounded like a great idea and that it was totally doable. She is thinking about doing it herself. We even talked about hosting a dinner together, with mindfulness as the theme, for our next book club meeting.

Emotional and physical states: That one day at work that I took my lunch outside, I noticed that I felt better and actually was able to feel when I started to get full. I liked being in tune with my body instead of feeling guilty after looking away from my computer screen for a moment only to see my empty Ziploc bag, not even knowing I inhaled my sandwich like I do most days at work. I noticed I enjoyed not only the meal that much more, but I also just enjoyed my afternoon more. I think it's because I took some time to myself to just mentally check out from work for a few moments and connect with nature a bit. My mind and my body felt more at ease, and

I was relaxed. I think if I did this more often, I might feel more comfortable in my body and in my mind in other areas of my life, too. I also feel pretty good that my friend thinks I can do this and that she might want to try to do it with me. I like the camaraderie in that. That way we can talk about what works and what doesn't, and maybe even have more dinners to enjoy together. And that makes me happier just knowing I can spend more quality time with her.

So you see, this theory can work for any type of behavior change. It is about checking into your head and really noticing how your body feels, then identifying interventions in each of these four areas to support your growth efforts.

Now it is your turn, one last time. Yes, my issue was about driving, but lots of folks have anxiety about things like taking tests, being in small spaces, being in large crowds, going to the dentist, being alone, spiders, swimming in a lake where you can't see the bottom; you name it, there's a phobia for it. Think about something that makes you uncomfortable that you might want to change. Is there something you avoid, that scares you, or that you just want to change in general? Or, if you really don't have any scary stuff that you need to or want to work on at this time, just think about something from our dimensions of wellness work and what opportunities you listed there, or one of the examples you used for the TTM or HBM earlier in this chapter. Maybe you want to be more in tune with Mother Nature, drink more water every day, or start volunteering in your community. The sky's the limit, my friends. Think about a potential behavior change that might interest you and apply that to the Self-Efficacy Theory.

Mastery experience:

Vicarious experience:

Verbal persuasion:

Physical and emotional states:

As we already chatted about, there are a ton of things that can influence your current health, health outcomes, and health-related choices: things like socioeconomic status, genetics, where you live, your neighborhood, ACEs, your culture, religion, societal norms, stress levels, education, values, beliefs, attitudes, and so much more are all influencers for change or lack thereof. This book is just a small sliver, an introduction into behavior change to get you started on your journey. You can deepen your knowledge by reading the additional resources at the end of this book or working with a health professional like a certified health coach to help you with the day-to-day minutia of behavior change. Hopefully this is giving you a good foundation from which to leap, though!

The show must go on!

In Chapter Eight we are going to the next level. We will work on setting concrete goals for you to achieve, now that you have all of this great information just waiting to be used!

CHAPTER EIGHT

WRITING YOUR FUTURE SCRIPT

Now that we have all of the information we need to get started on the path to sustainable behavior change, we need to think about how we get from our current story line to the future story line by actually writing a script. Let's face it, impromptu ad-libbing can be all good and fun to watch on stage, but there are very few of us that are talented enough to shoot from the hip and actually pull it off well. Most of us need some structure to be successful. In this chapter, we will have a discussion on values and beliefs and how to align those with thoughts and behaviors to help you goal set. We will work together to set goals in a **SMART** format to easily measure your successes, or to help you refocus in a compassionate manner when life gets in the way. Finally, we will discuss setting intentions without clinging to expectations to support that newfound inner cheerleader. See ya later, Nellie!

First things first. Let's check in and see how you are feeling about this behavior change stuff. It can be a tad bit overwhelming, so we are going to break it down into digestible chunks together. Let's revisit our values. Go ahead and list your top five values that you indicated on page 131.

Values:

Recall from your past notations or brainstorm a different behavior change that you think you want to try in the next couple of weeks, big or small. Reflect back on our wellness dimension work or the behavior change theory examples we worked through in the last chapter for ideas to get you started. Write down your concept or initial idea here:

Then tell me how your values might potentially align with this chosen behavior change:

What is your "why"? Why is this behavior change important to you? What will help you continue the inspiration when the going gets tough? Remember, the whys are your intrinsic motivators;

this change is for you not for anyone else. Tell me, in your gut, why is this change important to you?

Now I want you to indicate what your beliefs are in terms of sustainable behavior change. How much do you believe in yourself to be able to make a change within the next few weeks? Measure this on a scale of 1 to 4, with 1 being Piglet's perceived ability to bounce and 4 being Tigger's perceived ability to bounce. This is your self-efficacy.

1 2 3 4

Now I want you to list some ideas of why you rated yourself the way you did. Include any reservations, potential barriers, pros/cons, and excitement you have surrounding the idea of behavior change. This is your decisional balance.

Reservations, hesitancies, worries:

_____

_____

_____

Potential barriers you might come up against:

_____

_____

_____

Physical and emotional excitement about this potential change and its effects:

_____

_____

_____

Support you have to make this change (unicorns, family, physical, emotional, and financial resources, etc.)

_____

_____

_____

Pros and cons of making this change:

_____

_____

_____

Do your pros, supports, and level of excitement outweigh the reservations and barriers at this time?

Yes   No   Maybe, I'm not sure yet

How ready are you to make this change? Circle one:

Precontemplation (I don't think I can change right now)

Contemplation Stage (just thinking about this)

Preparation Stage (I am getting ready and taking baby steps to make the action)

*If you answered "no," you are probably in the precontemplation stage. If you answered "maybe/not sure," you are probably in the contemplation stage. If you answered "yes," you are probably in the preparation stage.

Excellent work! It can be challenging to get real with yourself in concrete terms. You are pretty darn brave right now. Remember that you increase your likelihood that the change will stick if:

- Your identified potential change aligns with your values
- You have a higher self-efficacy, meaning you rated yourself closer to Tigger in your belief in yourself
- You map out potential barriers and worries and identify ways to combat those before you start
- Your pros outweigh your cons
- You are clear about your "why(s)" for the change
- You create an intervention that matches your stage of readiness to change
- You map out the change in concrete terms
- You secure support from unicorns and have resources to support the change

Now that you have laid out in black and white what your headspace is and how you feel about this change, let's take some actionable steps to narrow your focus and increase your chances of success in doing so. We are going to do this by creating a goal. Keep in mind that goals are different from values, yet they are intrinsically linked (or at least should be). Goals are measurable; they change as we change. Values typically tend to stick with us; they demonstrate the qualities and characteristics that make us who we are. Goals can be better achieved if they align with our values. Values guide our actions; actions help us meet our goals.

When we ensure that our goals and actions are values-driven, we will have less suffering and lead a more meaningful life.

The best way to execute any change, be it drinking more water or climbing Mount Everest, is to write a script; aka, have a plan. In this section we are going to write a detailed script to keep you on track. First, I want you to recall the potential barriers or worries you might have about attempting this behavior change. Then I want you to brainstorm ideas on how you might be able to overcome those obstacles.

Let me start you off with an example. I value living in a vibrant and healthy community. My goal is to volunteer in my community more. My worries are that I don't have enough time to dedicate to that commitment, that I won't find something that I am passionate enough about to follow through with this goal, or that I will volunteer and not "jive" with the people or the organization. My barriers are that I have a busy work schedule and I am responsible for caring for both my children and my aging parents, which limits my time commitment ability.

To improve the odds of success of achieving my volunteerism goal, I need to keep these considerations in mind as I map out my plan. In this example, time is a big deal, followed by passion and human connection as potential pitfalls. Keeping these considerations in mind during my preparation stage of behavior change, I am going to acknowledge that these things could potentially decrease my chances of success, because ignoring time constraints and emotions surrounding the "extra" stuff I am putting on my plate will only set me up for failure. I might be able to do it the first month or two because I am excited about volunteering and how it will impact my health and the health of my community, but as the excitement fades, that will not be sustainable as the realities of life set in. So to address these barriers, I could do the following during my preparations:

- Look on the local United Way or community website to see who needs what type of volunteer for their organizations. Most will list what the organization is and what they do, what the volunteering activities are, and what the time commitment could be. Using these tools, I can help identify what would align with my interests, talents, and time constraints.
- Look at my schedule to see realistically how much more I can take on. Maybe twice a month is unrealistic now that soccer is starting, and my parents are needing more clinic visits. Maybe I should look to volunteer at one-time events like a 5K or other community gathering in order to decrease the commitment level, at least initially, while I try to figure out how to work this into my regular routine.
- Ask at the organizations that I am already involved with if they need help. Maybe Joey's soccer team needs a person to help organize the fundraiser, or maybe the local Aging and Disability Resource Center where my parents attend fall prevention classes needs some help with administrative work. If I am already engaged with the organization, then I know I already have an affinity for it in some way, and I might even know some of the people and hence know that I "jive" with them and their organizational mission. And if I don't know anyone at these organizations, then it might be a good idea to get to know some of the folks there.
- Identify some organizations that need help where I can include my parents and/or my kids in the volunteerism. Perhaps my church needs help decorating for the holiday

season or the local YMCA needs help with yard work to ready their camp for the summer session. By making this a family affair, I can kill two birds with one stone by spending quality time with loved ones and helping my community. It can teach my kids the value of volunteerism, too.

Now it's your turn. Based on the worries and barriers you listed for your potential behavior change, what are some interventions that you might be able to employ to avoid those pitfalls and make the behavior change easier to adopt in a sustainable fashion?

Now that you have honed your goal to meet your values and beliefs and to avoid any potential problems, we need to write your goal in a way that is concrete. The only way you will know if you are successful or not is to have a measurable goal. There is no way you could know for sure if you scored a field goal or not if you didn't have a goal post. There is no way to know for sure if you finished that 10K without the finish line or your MapMyRun app telling you in concrete terms that you made it 6.2 miles. We will use a goal writing tool so that you know exactly where that success lies and what it looks like so you can celebrate your accomplishments or recalibrate to make things more achievable when life gets in the way. We do that by creating SMART goals. SMART is an acronym for the guidelines we will use in creating these goals. It stands for:

S	Specific	You need to be very clear about what exactly you want to do. Include "W's" like who, what, why, where, or when, and don't forget the "H": how
M	Measurable	How much and/or how often
A	Achievable	Can you realistically accomplish this? Think about all of your pros and cons, your readiness to change, self-efficacy, and how it will fit into your life, avoiding pitfalls
R	Relevant	Does it align with your values, beliefs, and your "why"?
T	Time-bound	You need an expiration date and/or a concrete timeline; what is the end date so that you can check in and see if you have met your measurable goal?

First, I am going to give you an example of a goal that is written in a not-so-great fashion and then I will flip it around to be in SMART format so that you can see the difference.

> Not-so-great goal writing example: I want to lose weight before my class reunion.
>
> SMART goal example: I want to lose ten pounds by July 1 by increasing my cardio to 30 minutes every other day and decreasing my caloric intake by 100 calories each day.

You see, if I just say that I want to lose weight, that could mean two pounds or 200 pounds. If I say I want to lose it before my class reunion, that could mean by the day of the reunion or by the week before so I still have time to go out buy a new outfit; or it could mean by my 25th reunion instead of my 20th reunion. By explicitly saying ten pounds, I know exactly how much, and by saying I want to lose that by July 1, I also am clear on the exact time frame. I can then follow those interventions like decreasing my calories and increasing my cardio to start working toward that goal. Saying ten pounds is specific, measurable, and achievable, whereas 200 pounds probably would not be realistic in a short amount of time (unless you are shooting for next year's reunion!). By saying July 1, this is time-bound; I know exactly where that goal post is. It is relevant if it aligns with my values and beliefs, coincides with my self-efficacy levels (how confident I am in my ability to do this), and reflects where I am at mentally in the stages of change. So if I am just toying with the idea of losing ten pounds (contemplation stage) instead of actively readying for that, such as in the preparation stage, I may want to amend that goal to read something like: "I will investigate different eating patterns, start reading food labels, and set up a MyFitnessPal account in the next two weeks to get a better sense of what I need to do for future weight loss." The contemplation stage is about gathering information to inform your decision making, whereas the preparation stage is actually preparing yourself and your environment and making baby steps toward that change when change is imminent. Make sense?

Let me offer you a few more examples of SMART goals so that you can get a better idea of what they look like for future reference. Next you will find an example of a SMART goal for each of the dimensions of wellness we reviewed previously. I have also included some preparation activities for each of the goals so that you can brainstorm preemptive interventions to support sustainable success in your chosen goal.

Environmental Dimension

I will purchase eggs from a local farmer and recycle my egg cartons for the remainder of this year to lessen my factory farm and waste footprint beginning this weekend.

Preparation activities to ready you for this goal:

I will make a space on top of my refrigerator to store the egg cartons that will be recycled.

I will ask my roommates if they want to buy farm fresh eggs, too. Maybe we can get a discount if we buy more at a time.

I will ask my friends and the vendors at the farmer's market which farmers sell eggs and what their pickup location is to ensure it is close for me and thus easy to access on a regular basis.

I will make a connection with a local farmer to pick up two dozen eggs one time per week on my day off.

Emotional Dimension

I will meditate five out of seven days each week for the month of June, for a minimum of five minutes each day, beginning next week.

Preparation activities to ready you for this goal:

I will ask friends and family who meditate for pointers on how to be successful.

I will try different apps on my phone and watch YouTube videos to see which ones I prefer.

I will block five minutes out of my lunchtime work schedule Monday through Friday to save this space for meditation and not allow meeting requests during this time.

I will add an auto response to my email during this time so that I am not disturbed during my meditation time.

Occupational Dimension

I will volunteer one time per month at my local food pantry for a total of one hour for each opportunity starting in June and ending in August before school starts back up again.

Preparation activities to ready you for this goal:

I will talk with the volunteer coordinator, tour the pantry, and shadow a person that is volunteering there to get a better understanding of what will be expected of me.

I will ask a friend to volunteer with me; maybe we can carpool.

I will sign up for a one-hour shift next month when I am touring the food pantry.

I will add the volunteer shift to my work and home schedules so as to not book any other appointments during that time.

Social Dimension

I will join my local neighborhood watch group and attend the monthly meetings beginning next month for a minimum of three months.

Preparation activities to ready you for this goal:

I will call my neighbor who is in charge of the neighborhood watch to express my interest and learn more about joining.

I will add the next month's meeting to my calendar and also invite my partner to join me.

I will introduce myself to neighbors I have not met yet and talk with them about the neighborhood watch group to see if others will want to join with me.

I will sign up for one shift of the watch along with another neighbor after I complete my first meeting.

Physical Dimension

Beginning on Saturday, for the next two weeks, I will stretch two times per week before bed for a total of ten minutes each time, making sure to stretch all of my upper body muscle groups one day and my lower body muscle groups the opposite day.

Preparation activities to ready you for this goal:

I will add a fitness app to my phone and start marking stretching video "favorites" in my account that include both upper and lower body stretches and total at least ten minutes in length.

I will set an alarm on my phone for 9 pm every night to remind me to stretch.

I will lay my yoga pants out on the chair next to my bed on top of my pjs so that I change into those clothes first before I ready myself for bed.

I will explain to my kids that I am doing this for my health so that I can continue to run around and play with them without pain. I will let them know that they can join me if they want to, but to not disturb me during this time if they choose to not join me.

Intellectual Dimension

I will stay on top of current events by reading at least three major headlines on my phone news app three times per week starting next week through the end of the month.

Preparation activities to ready you for this goal:

I will research which news organizations have the least amount of bias and which news organizations outside of my home country offer unbiased reporting.

I will download two different balanced news apps on my phone, one national and one international.

I will talk with my partner about the current events I have read about over breakfast in the morning.

I will sign up for an email from one of the organizations to get the top headlines delivered to me daily.

Spiritual Dimension

I will connect with Mother Nature by taking a walk one time each weekend with my kids, beginning next weekend until school starts back up again.

Preparation activities to ready you for this goal:

I will read stories to and talk with my children about the importance of appreciating nature and how that helps our health.

I will find three parks within walking distance of our home that are family friendly and have nature trails.

I will join an online hiking group in my local area to help me locate different trails for our weekend trips.

I will buy hiking boots for myself and my children.

Financial Dimension

I will save $50 out of each paycheck starting on January 1 and ending on December 31 and place that money in a separate vacation account so that I do not go into credit card debt again with my next vacation.

Preparation activities to ready you for this goal:

I will review my finances and monthly bills with my partner to ensure that I/we can comfortably set this aside out of each paycheck.

I will set up the coffee pot at home each evening and put it on a timer so that it brews right away in the morning. That way I can drink less expensive home brews instead of stopping at the coffee shop every morning; this will help me to pay for this new vacation budget allocation without really feeling it.

I will stop at my bank to complete the paperwork for a separate vacation savings account.

I will talk with and submit the paperwork to my HR representative to set up an auto-draft to my new account directly from my paycheck.

I hope you can see the SMART pattern within these goals. Remember, the more concrete and measurable you make these goals, the easier you will know when you have accomplished something and be proud of that sustained change. Listing out your preparation activities can help you be successful in avoiding potential pitfalls (barriers to success) and achieving sustainability.

While this planning tool is a great start, you also need to be flexible and allow yourself to go back to the drawing board sometimes. There may be barriers that happen along the way that you do not or cannot plan for. That vacation account sounds great now, but what happens if your partner loses her job? The wilderness hiking looks great on paper, but what happens if your child develops an outdoor allergy? Give yourself the space and the grace to let go of rigidity and rework your goals. Maybe the vacation account needs to be put on hold until your partner finds a new job. Maybe your kiddo does better hiking in the winter instead of during ragweed season. This is life. Stuff happens. Remember that mindfulness conversation we had? Allowing the experience to play out without pushing it away or clinging to it is a key component of mindfulness; the same thing holds true for your goal setting, because sometimes you might not be able to accomplish what you initially set out to achieve the way you initially conceptualized it. The same thing holds true on the flip side, too. Perhaps you are a rockstar with your stretching routine and figure out that you absolutely love doing it. You might love it so much that you revisit that goal and add on to it by actually joining a yoga studio and participating in a group fitness community three days a week in addition to your ten-minute bedtime stretch that has now become routine. That is fabulous; go with it! We are all constantly assessing and reassessing to figure out how we can be the best versions of ourselves at any given moment. Big or small, stumbles or successes; it doesn't matter, just keep working toward forward progress and continuous quality improvement. Unless you achieve enlightenment. Then I think you're good to go.

OK, after all of that information, it is your turn once more! Let's have you write this script! I want you to revisit your idea for a behavior change that you can do relatively soon. Again, if you are not ready for change, that is fine. You can certainly set goals for yourself even if you are in the contemplation stage. Recall that contemplation stage goals would be more information-seeking in nature. Now, tell me what your goal is and what your preparation activities would be to get you ready for that behavior change. Keep in mind any barriers and worries that you listed. Some of the preparation activities should address those potential pitfalls.

Behavior change goal in **SMART** format:

I will:

My preparation activities to get me ready for this change and avoid barriers include:

I will:

How are you feeling about all of this? Does this seem doable to you? Realistic? Are you excited? Now that you have this all scripted out in black and white staring you in the face, I want to ask you one more time what your beliefs are in terms of sustainable behavior change in regard to this SMART goal. How much do you believe in yourself to be able to make this change? What is your level of self-efficacy?

Measure on a scale of 1 to 4 with 1 being Piglet's perceived ability to bounce and 4 being Tigger's perceived ability to bounce.

1 2 3 4

Did your self-efficacy level change at all after reworking your ideas into a SMART format?

Yes   No

Why did you choose yes or no? Just jot down some ideas on why that might be.

If you chose yes, excellent. I am happy you are more comfortable with how your change idea is taking shape. If you chose no, then you might need to consider setting a more realistic goal for yourself. It could be that the change you initially chose feels too overwhelming, not achievable or sustainable, or you're simply just not ready. If that is the case, just break it up into a smaller chunk, a baby step if you will. You might be in the contemplation stage instead of the preparation stage. Or you might be in the precontemplation stage instead of the contemplation stage. No big deal, just step it back a bit and reassess where you are right now. If you attempt to do too much too soon, it will most often end up not working out, and that will just decrease your self-efficacy for the next time you are toying with the idea of a change. There are many different things that can influence your ability to change; it's not just about that burning desire in your belly right now. Things like your social dynamic, your finances, the people that surround you, your cultural norms, and your environment can all impact your ability to achieve a goal. Once more, here's an example to illustrate what I mean.

If your goal is to learn how to belly dance, but as you're writing out your barriers you realize belly dancing is something that is not socially or culturally accepted in your family circle, you may feel like this goal is dead on arrival due to lack of support, or maybe you are just worried you may experience some outward criticism or opposition to the idea. You are going to need to address this potential barrier first before forging ahead with signing up for a class. Instead of giving up on the idea totally, you might want to amend your goal to simply broach the topic and have a conversation with your partner or family members about belly dancing so as to investigate what their attitudes are toward it and why they hold those attitudes. Simply learning more about their cultural attitudes and beliefs that surround this topic might impact your future goal of participating in a belly dancing class. Maybe during the conversation you could find a workaround or a compromise that makes everyone happy and that could lead to a new scriptwriting process to achieve your goal. I used sort of a lighthearted example here, but there could be some sensitive goals you have that might align with your values but not the values, attitudes, and beliefs of those that are close to you. When brainstorming your potential barriers, it is important to think about not only the barriers as you see them, but how others that impact your life will perceive and receive your change. Here are some more challenging examples to get you thinking. If you want to quit smoking but your partner smokes and has no desire to quit, this can be a significant influencer on your behavior and your ability to be successful. If you want to limit how much you drink but your bestie doesn't want to give up "Thirsty Thursdays" each week, it might be harder for you to limit your Moscow Mule intake. If you want your kids to stop eating so much sugar by not buying Oreos and Fudgsicles, but your partner keeps bringing these items home from the store, this is going to influence your ability to adopt and sustain the change. Behavior change does not occur in a vacuum; there are many considerations when trying to adopt a new behavior. Rarely are those considerations all about you; actions have consequences that affect those around us, both good and bad.

Have you considered some of those cultural, social, economic, environmental, attitudinal, and belief issues that might act as barriers to your sustained behavior change efforts from those that are closest to you? What could potentially create a plot twist that you don't want to happen? Brainstorm that list and write them down here:

The art of negotiation is important, but another consideration to sustaining your change is seeking, planning, and securing support for yourself. You don't have to be passive and give up on your desires if there are some conflicts like what you noted earlier. Even if your partner is willing to smoke outside instead of inside, or keep the Oreos at the office instead of at home, you still need to seek out and secure strong environmental and social-emotional support from others when embarking upon behavior change. Have conversations with those that you believe will be supportive of you and what you are planning. Not only will that increase your accountability to the change, but they can help you! Buddy system! Securing social and emotional support from loved ones (aka unicorn cheerleaders) can be that extra cushion when you are feeling down, you stumble, or you stagnate on your progress, and environmental support will offer you the cues to make the change easier to sustain. In my examples of preparation activities for corresponding SMART goals earlier, I embedded some social-emotional support and environmental cue activities as examples to show you how to make the change process easier. I will highlight those here.

Social and Emotional Support Preparation Activities

I will ask my roommates if they want to buy farm fresh eggs, too. Maybe we can get a discount if we buy more at a time.

I will ask a friend to volunteer with me; maybe we can carpool.

I will call my neighbor who is in charge of the neighborhood watch to express my interest and learn more about joining.

I will introduce myself to neighbors I have not met yet and talk with them about the neighborhood watch group to see if others will want to join with me.

I will explain to my kids that I am doing this for my health so that I can continue to run around and play with them without pain. I will let them know that they can join me if they want to, but to not disturb me during this time if they choose to not join me.

I will talk with my partner about the current events I have read about over breakfast in the morning.

I will join an online hiking group in my local area to help me locate different trails for our weekend trips.

I will review my finances and monthly bills with my partner to ensure that I/we can comfortably set this aside out of each paycheck.

Environmental Cue Preparation Activities

I will make a space on top of my refrigerator to store the egg cartons that will be recycled.

I will block five minutes out of my lunchtime work schedule Monday through Friday to save this space for meditation and not allow meeting requests during this time.

I will add an auto response to my email during this time so that I am not disturbed during my meditation time.

I will add the volunteer shift to my work and home schedules so as to not book any other appointments during that time.

I will lay my yoga pants out on the chair next to my bed on top of my pjs so that I change into those clothes first before I ready myself for bed.

I will sign up for an email from one of the organizations to get the top headlines delivered to me daily.

I will buy hiking boots for myself and my children.

I will set up the coffee pot at home each evening and put it on a timer so that it brews right away in the morning. That way I can drink less expensive home brews instead of stopping at the coffee shop every morning; this will help me to pay for this new vacation budget allocation without really feeling it.

So the social-emotional support gives you the boots-on-the-ground, real-time help from folks to help you stay accountable, and the environmental cues are those physical things that make the change sustainable by incorporating it into your everyday life with ease, or at least less resistance. Here is a golden nugget for sustainable behavior change: you always want to make the healthy choice the easy choice.

Here we go. First, I want you to think about who your cheerleaders are and who can help you make this change easier and more sustainable. Friends, family, partners, neighbors, co-workers . . .

whoever might be able to influence the outcome of this change. And be realistic about this. Just because your BFF is your BFF doesn't mean she will necessarily help in your endeavor. I'm not saying your BFF is a bad person, but sometimes the comfort zone is just more, well, comfy for folks. Let's say your goal is to drink less alcohol, but whenever you and your bestie get together, you each end up downing a bottle of wine. Will your bestie be OK with taking the doggos for a walk instead of having cocktails on the patio? Or does she see no need to change and likes things status quo? If she isn't going to support your change, you might not want to give her center-stage seats to this event. Seek out and secure those that will help you. Who are your people that can help you make this change and make it stick? Who can help you stay accountable? Who in your life can make this easier? Who will help you pick yourself up and dust you off if you stumble or fall flat on your nose? List them here:

_____

_____

_____

_____

Next up are those environmental cues. What can you do to make this change easier and support a more seamless transition to habit formation? Is it packing your gym bag and putting it in your car before you leave for work each day? Avoiding the liquor section of the grocery store? Creating an electronic fund transfer to start saving more? Think about the environmental preparatory cues that can help you support this change after the excitement and "newness" wears off. The less you have to think about the change, the better. Make it easier for yourself by creating an environment that supports you and your effort. List the environmental cues you can create to support your behavior change by making the healthy choice the easy choice.

The show must go on!

You have done so much work writing your future script for your Act Two; I am so proud of you! Now before we move on to the last chapter, I want you to get up, move, and think for a while. Stop reading. Go do a load of laundry, go for a walk, make dinner, chat with a friend on the phone, and just decompress. This is a lot of stuff to put together. We have covered so much content in a very short amount of time together. Ruminating on all of these concepts for a spell can help bring them together, like a good marinade for your chicken. You want it to sit for a bit to marry before you throw Cluck Norris on the grill. Give your *pollo* some bath time and I will meet you back here for the last chapter so we can stitch this all together.

CHAPTER NINE

CURTAIN CALL

Earlier I asked the question, "Who are you and what is your story?" Do you have an answer? Has your answer changed at all? Now I have a few more questions for you.

- Do you have a clearer understanding of where you have been, why you are where you are right now, and what kind of plan you might have for your future?
- Do you have a deeper appreciation for what it means to be healthy, and the interrelated nature of the different dimensions and determinants?
- Do you appreciate and embrace that you are the best decision maker/influencer/leading role and narrator for your own life?

It is my hope that you have a firmer understanding of these topics and have a good start on some answers for these questions.

One of my friends used to tell me that her health goals sounded fantastic on Friday evenings with an adult beverage in hand while soaking in her hot tub, but come Monday when the rubber met the road, life would get in the way and the tires would start to fall off the car. The journey to achieving goals becomes more difficult as those barriers that weren't on the radar (life happens kinda stuff!) appear. But when we offer ourselves the space to understand that life will get in the way sometimes, we can more easily rebound and amend our goals to make sure our intentions actually align with and can fit into our daily life. Let go of the rigidity, but still keep that "why" in mind to continue your momentum in meeting your goal in one fashion or another.

Before we part ways, I wanted to share just one more of my stories with you. As you are well aware by now, I started a meditation practice to help my panic attack issue. Well, I have shared the successes so far, but not many of my opportunities for growth that I experienced along the way. Here goes.

When I first started meditating, I was quite the skeptic. I really did not know how I could sit still for anything longer than 60 seconds. It felt unfathomable and out of reach to me, and for those that know me well, I am certain they would concur. I started off with a goal of just learning more about the topic and hoping that maybe I could actually sit for a minute or two at a time without going mad. I began first with reading the initial book that I chose to guide my path (preparation phase). Then I purchased the annual subscription for my chosen app and gave it a whirl. It was sort of fits and spurts in the beginning. Whenever I would think about meditating, make the time, and feel like I had the capacity to sit still, I would try it out. The app I chose had many courses that actually taught me about meditation, what the point of it was, what was happening behind the scenes, how to not feel like a failure, what success really looked like, what to actually "do" during the sit time, and so on. It was highly beneficial for me. As I began to learn more about the practice, I began to appreciate that this was not going to be a quick fix. This was not like taking a pill and making my symptoms go away; rather it was a commitment to whittling away at the issue slowly, to cure it with patience (which is most assuredly not my virtue of choice). I was assured by teachers in these courses that I wouldn't really notice a big change from a meditation practice until I was practicing for a while and was "tested" by real life. This test would come in the form of a difficult life challenge and instead of emotionally reacting to it, I would respond to it rationally. Of course I didn't really understand what these teachers meant, until "it" happened. The first time I noticed what that success looked like, I still lost control of my emotions for a bit, but not for as long as I normally would have, and I didn't cling to the anger that was aroused in me for as long as I normally would have. In subsequent times I was able to actually see my anger rising, name it, frame it, accept it, and then process it without a scene. I was literally able to say with my inside voice, "This is what anger feels like"; I allowed it, responded to it, and "it" worked. I didn't let the emotion take over me and my actions. Now, I am not saying I don't lose it anymore. I totally do. I'm human. It happens. However, losing it is a little less intense, less frequent, and doesn't last as long. I am a little bit less of a jerk and I rebound from the stressful event more quickly than I would have without this practice. I don't ruminate for weeks on what transpired, reliving the scene over and over again. I can let it go. I can apologize. I can talk about it. So, it took patience, practice, time, and all of those other things we talked about in this book to make my practice a habit that changed my behaviors in a positive and sustainable way.

Here is a specific example of how the meditation practice helped me through an issue. I am a very goal-centric kind of gal. I will create these artificial due dates or goals for myself and once I do, I typically meet them. Well, one of my goals was a streak. No, not that kind of "streak." I wanted to meditate for 365 days straight using my meditation app. I was so on task for this. I never missed a day, no matter how crazy life got. I always took the time for myself to get it done. Well, then the great Thanksgiving Day debacle occurred. I was busy, busy, busy getting the house cleaned and the meal prepped all day long. Then everyone came over, we had a lovely meal, and after everyone went home, I quickly crawled into bed because I was exhausted. You guessed it: no meditation that day. I woke up at 2 am with a start, realizing what I had done.

I opened my app and sure enough, the streak was back down to zero. I had been within just a few short weeks of my year-long goal. But here is where the magically delicious marshmallows and milk come together, my friends! When I first made this realization, honestly, I was pretty upset. Then I thought to myself:

- This is what disappointment, anger, and frustration feel like. (mindfulness)
- I am human, I make mistakes just like everyone else. (common humanity)
- I can forgive myself for this. It was an artificial goal that I made for myself. No harm, no foul. I made great progress toward it, and I have made great progress toward becoming a better version of me in the process and I am proud of that. It will be OK. (self-compassion practice)
- I made it almost a year, every day, and was successful at that. I can reboot this goal based on my lived experiences and make a new goal to start over and continue my forward momentum in helping me help myself. (self-efficacy and mastery experience)
- This will give me the opportunity to go back and review the courses to perhaps learn and understand more now that I have almost a year of daily practice under my belt. (growth mindset)

And you know what? New Carrie was able to go through this checklist in about ten minutes after the realization, recalibrate, and actually fall back asleep. Old Carrie would have been awake the rest of the night lamenting about how stupid of a mistake it was, and how much I had lost because of that one dumb screw-up, and I probably would have given up. I like the new Carrie better.

Knowing that I am goal centric and not wanting to leave behind this sustained behavior of meditation, I needed to recalibrate since life got in the way. So what was my new goal? To have 1,000 total days of meditation instead of a 365-day streak. This would support my forward progress in my practice, yet give me the flexibility to miss a day here and there in case anything life threw at me disrupted my flow. Did I bust that goal? You bet I did! Am I a healthier person because of it? You betcha.

I am a strong believer in "everything happens for a reason." I might not see it at the time, but I am almost always able to reflect back on a situation and find something positive or a "golden nugget" to better understand the when or why of how a situation unfolded. Listen to this, because I have a great example here, too! As it so happened, there were a few more days of meditation that I missed after rebooting from the great Thanksgiving Day debacle and creating the 1,000-day total goal instead of the streak goal. And I am so happy that I did, because Day 1,000 could not have been more perfect or fitting if I had tried. Day 1,000 came when I was in my happy place: Costa Rica. I was at this beautiful home in the mountainous region of Atenas. If you have never been there, I highly recommend a road trip, my friends.

Anyway, more storytelling to share with you. I had a very challenging travel day getting to Costa Rica. I had been looking forward to this trip for well over a year. Pandemic issues had delayed me for far too long, and on the day of travel we had many, many setbacks. At one point we were not even sure we would make it to Costa Rica that day. When we arrived at the airport for our first flight, after about an hour of waiting, we were told that the plane needed a new part, and we could not fly without it. We were flying out of a small regional airport in Wisconsin, so the airline mechanics had to wait for another plane to bring the part from Chicago O'Hare. That meant we were never going to make our connecting flight. We were able to rebook by adding another stop on our journey, which totaled three separate flights and meant getting into San José late at night, so we also needed to find someone to come pick us up at the airport since the car rental agency was only open until early evening. Thankfully we were able to connect with the owner of the home, who arranged for his friend Walter to pick us up when we arrived. After all of these schedule changes and updates to our itinerary, there was yet another setback. The next airline announcement notified us that with the wait for the part and the time it would take to replace the part, we might not even make our new connecting flight, which meant we would be staying the night in Charlotte, North Carolina, instead of Costa Rica. Now, folks from Charlotte, I have nothing against you, and I am certain your town is beautiful; however, when I had been anticipating Costa Rica for so long, it was a li'l bit of a letdown. Apologies.

At that point we had resigned ourselves to staying the night in Charlotte and we were OK with that, because the way we saw it, that meant we were making forward progress getting physically closer to Costa Rica, and we were still spending time together, which is priceless. But with the grace of Mother Universe shining down on us, we narrowly made each of our connecting flights and had Walter waiting (and waiting) at the San José airport to pick us up. By this time poor Walter had been there awhile, and we were nearing midnight due to yet another setback. We needed to take an unexpected and expensive trip to "room number 17" before we could go through customs because of some missing paperwork (my bad!). Needless to say, the day was absolutely fraught with challenges. But it made putting our feet on Costa Rican soil that night that much sweeter! Not one time did I lose it. My partner and I even laughed and hugged throughout the entire journey at the ridiculousness of it all. It was an adventure to say the least, because that is how we viewed it. I like this new Carrie so much better.

So back to my 1,000-day goal story. We finally arrived at our rental house in the middle of the night, drunk with exhaustion. We collapsed into bed and didn't wake until much later the next day. Upon waking, it was just a magical sight. The mountains, the birds, the forest . . . it was all worth the trepidation of the journey. I wandered downstairs to soak it all in and appreciate the innate beauty before me. I laid down on this typical Costa Rican wooden lounge chair on the patio, and opened up my meditation app to, you guessed it, the 1,000th sit. I meditated to the sounds of cows lowing, Mother Nature chatters, and iguanas skittering across the red clay-tiled roof above me. It was absolutely perfect. The great Thanksgiving Day debacle afforded me many opportunities and gifts, and this most certainly was a beautiful gift.

From the time I started this journey to now, I have come so far. All of those lessons and treasures along the way may not have felt like lessons and treasures at the time, but that is what they grew to be. Each was earned through tiny little life interventions over the course of several years, culminating in some big, positive steps forward in my health journey. You might be thinking, now what? You had this great meditative experience, you got to 1,000 and then some; what's the next goal? Well, I've gotta say, I'm not quite sure yet. I still use my app, but I am less dependent on it, and that is a good thing. It means that I have made sustainable lifestyle changes and these changes are just part of who I am now. I set my phone down more often and really listen when folks are talking to me. I can sit outside without preoccupation and appreciate the color of a bird's wings and the song they sing. I have quiet moments on my front porch appreciating the smell and taste of a cup of coffee, sitting close with my partner, watching the squirrels perform gymnastics as time slips past. I have more patience with myself and others (still not my favorite virtue, though). I can drive without panic. I can stop myself and ask the question "Is this useful?" when I get stuck in the infinite worry loop of potential future events or the lamenting of past events, and can then just let it go. I can help myself work through a panic attack. I'm a little bit less of a jerk to people that irk me. I lose my temper a little less often. I can breathe. I have found the feeling of contentment, and it feels great. I am renewed; a better version of me. I have reclaimed my spirit.

Knowing that I have these concrete, tangible changes to my health and well-being tells me that I do not need to use my app every day; I have taught myself through the use of the app how to do it all by myself. I am by no means a meditative guru, but I can sustain this practice. So I guess my goal is to maintain a meditative practice in my daily life in all those micro moments of opportunity.

I have a list of reminders for you as you venture off on your behavior change journey. You might not be ready for an actual **SMART** goal right at this moment, but perhaps you might be able to consider picking one or two things off of this list to get you moving in a forward motion, gaining momentum, and in turn increasing your self-efficacy for when you are ready to tackle that behavior change goal.

Checklist before we go:

- Have you turned off your autopilot and awakened to your inner dialogue?
- Have you begun to tame your inner critic?
- If you haven't tamed your inner critic, can you hijack it sometimes?
- Do you employ positive self-talk? How about on a regular basis?
- Have you swaddled yourself in unicorn love?
- Have you set your stage for behavior change by embracing positivity and belief in yourself and your ability to change for the better?
- Have you let go of the "I am good, or I am bad" false dichotomy?
- Have you forgiven yourself?
- Have you forgiven others?
- Have you let go of your fears? Or are you working on it?
- Have you embraced the notion of self-compassion?
- How's your gratitude practice coming along?
- Have you found your joy?
- Have you found your "why"?
- Are you mindful during your thoughts and actions toward yourself and others?
- Can you accept people, events, actions, and thoughts without judgment, or pushing away or clinging to them?
- Do you see challenges and setbacks as learning moments and renewed opportunities for growth?

Remember that your path to behavior change will be easier if you can accept and actively practice these considerations, but they are not required for successful change. They simply will serve as a solid foundation for you to launch from and lean on when the going gets tough. We are all works in progress; none of us have mastered this list, so do not feel like you can't attempt behavior change until you make it through this whole checklist.

One last time, I will ask you to put your pen to paper and write your script for your first behavior change. Then after you make this change a habit, you can use it as a template for other changes you would like to make.

Curtain close!

Recall the behavior change that you want to attempt. Keep in mind that the goal should align with the stage of change you are in (contemplation or preparation would be the two most likely if you've made it to the end of this book).

List your SMART (specific, measurable, achievable, relevant, time-bound) goal here:

Recall what your "why" is. Why are you doing this and why is it important to you? Write that here:

Go through the checklist on page 256. What are you doing well? Working on? Need more work on?

Doing well:

Working on:

On my future to-do list:

List the preparation activities that will help increase the success of the identified behavior change here. Be sure to have at least one preparatory activity for (a) any potential barriers you might come up against, like time, financial, social, cultural, etc., (b) any potential barriers that you might come up against from those that have influence over your behaviors, (c) securing social and emotional support for when you need help, and (d) addressing environmental cues to make it easier for you to sustain the change.

List your supporting actors and who specifically you can lean on for help when the director threatens to swap you out for the understudy:

What does "success" look like for you?

___

Standing O!

And there you have it, folks! That's a wrap! You should be so proud of yourself; that was a lot of work. But despite curtain calls and your standing O, truly, the show must go on! You now have your script, your props, your people, everything needed to make your story a blockbuster success. It is up to you to make the magic happen. With behavior change, it is best to take a "go slow and you'll go far" attitude, coupled with embracing the good ol' Pollyanna mindset and letting poor ol' Negative Nellie fade away in the background. A large part of this process boils down to positivity in your headspace and in your attitude toward yourself. Be kind to yourself; it really does matter. Happiness is an inside job. Renew yourself. Reclaim your spirit. Be well, my friends.

ENCORE

ADDITIONAL READING TO FURTHER SUPPORT YOUR INTELLECTUAL HEALTH AND WELL-BEING

Generalized "Go-To" Resources for Medical, Health, and Wellness Information

Berkeley Greater Good Science Center: https://greatergood.berkeley.edu/

Centers for Disease Control and Prevention (CDC): https://www.cdc.gov/

Harvard Health Publishing: https://www.health.harvard.edu/

Mayo Clinic: https://www.mayoclinic.org/

National Institutes of Health (NIH): https://www.nih.gov/

The National Wellness Institute: https://nationalwellness.org/

Robert Wood Johnson Foundation Health Policy in Brief: https://www.rwjf.org/en/library/collections/health-policy-in-brief.html

U.S. Department of Health and Human Services: https://www.hhs.gov/

World Health Organization (WHO): https://www.who.int/

Meditation Resources

American Heart Association: Meditation to Boost Health and Well-Being: https://www.heart.org/en/healthy-living/healthy-lifestyle/mental-health-and-wellbeing/meditation-to-boost-health-and-wellbeing

Berkeley: Five Ways Mindfulness Meditation Is Good for Your Health: https://greatergood.berkeley.edu/article/item/five_ways_mindfulness_meditation_is_good_for_your_health

Harvard: What Meditation Can Do For Your Mind, Mood, and Health: https://www.health.harvard.edu/staying-healthy/what-meditation-can-do-for-your-mind-mood-and-health-

Mayo Clinic: Meditation: A Simple, Fast Way to Reduce Stress: https://www.mayoclinic.org/tests-procedures/meditation/in-depth/meditation/art-20045858

NIH: 8 Things to Know About Meditation for Health: https://www.nccih.nih.gov/health/tips/things-to-know-about-meditation-for-health

NIH: Meditation: In Depth: https://www.nccih.nih.gov/health/meditation-in-depth

UC Davis Health: 10 Health Benefits of Meditation: https://health.ucdavis.edu/news/headlines/10-health-benefits-of-meditation/2019/06

Self-Compassion Practice Resources

Kristen Neff: https://self-compassion.org/

University of California Berkeley Greater Good Science Center. (2021). *What is forgiveness?* Greater Good Magazine. https://greatergood.berkeley.edu/topic/forgiveness/definition

Loving Kindness Meditation Practice Resources

Berkeley: Loving-Kindness Meditation: https://ggia.berkeley.edu/practice/loving_kindness_meditation

Sharon Salzberg: https://www.sharonsalzberg.com/

Social Determinants of Health and Health Equity Resources

American Academy of Family Practice: Advancing Health Equity by Addressing the Social Determinants of Health in Family Medicine (Position Paper): https://www.aafp.org/about/policies/all/social-determinants-health-family-medicine-position-paper.html

American Public Health Association: Health Equity: https://www.apha.org/topics-and-issues/health-equity

CDC: Adverse Childhood Experiences (ACEs): https://www.cdc.gov/vitalsigns/aces/index.html and https://www.cdc.gov/violenceprevention/aces/index.html

CDC. (2022, April 6). *Fast facts: preventing adverse childhood experiences.* https://www.cdc.gov/violenceprevention/aces/fastfact.html#:~:text=How%20big%20is%20the%20problem,potentially%20reduce%20many%20health%20conditions

CDC: Health Equity: https://www.cdc.gov/chronicdisease/healthequity/index.htm

CDC: Health Equity: https://www.cdc.gov/healthequity/index.html

CDC: Social Determinants of Health: https://www.cdc.gov/chronicdisease/programs-impact/sdoh.htm

Kaiser Family Foundation: The Role of Social Determinants in Promoting Health and Health Equity: https://www.kff.org/racial-equity-and-health-policy/issue-brief/beyond-health-care-the-role-of-social-determinants-in-promoting-health-and-health-equity/

Robert Wood Johnson Foundation: Life Expectancy: https://www.rwjf.org/en/library/interactives/whereyouliveaffectshowlongyoulive.html

United Way: United for ALICE: https://www.unitedforalice.org/national-overview

University of Wisconsin Population Health Institute, School of Medicine and Public Health: County Health Rankings Data: https://www.countyhealthrankings.org/

Virginia Commonwealth University: Mapping Life Expectancy: https://societyhealth.vcu.edu/work/the-projects/mapping-life-expectancy.html

WHO: Social Determinants of Health: https://www.who.int/health-topics/social-determinants-of-health#tab=tab_1

Genetics and Epigenetics Resources

CDC: Genetics Basics: https://www.cdc.gov/genomics/about/basics.htm

CDC: What is Epigenetics?: https://www.cdc.gov/genomics/disease/epigenetics.htm#:~:text=Epigenetics%20is%20the%20study%20of,body%20reads%20a%20DNA%20sequence

MedlinePlus: Genetics: https://medlineplus.gov/genetics/

MedlinePlus: What is Epigenetics?: https://medlineplus.gov/genetics/understanding/howgeneswork/epigenome/

National Human Genome Research Institute: Child Abuse Leaves Epigenetic Marks: https://www.genome.gov/child-abuse-leaves-epigenetic-marks

National Human Genome Research Institute: Studying Cancer From the Inside Out: What the Epigenetic Code Can Tell Doctors About Disease: https://www.genome.gov/news/news-release/Studying-cancer-from-the-inside-out-What-the-epigenetic-code-can-tell-doctors-about-disease

National Library of Medicine: Epigenetics: The Science of Change: https://www.ncbi.nlm.nih.gov/pmc/articles/PMC1392256/

National Library of Medicine: Genetics and Health: https://www.ncbi.nlm.nih.gov/books/NBK19932/

National Library of Medicine: The Science of Epigenetics: https://www.ncbi.nlm.nih.gov/pmc/articles/PMC2861525/

PBS: Epigenetics: https://ideastream.pbslearningmedia.org/asset/biot09_vid_epigenetics/

PBS: Study Finds PTSD Effects May Linger in Body Chemistry of Next Generation: https://youtu.be/zV9sya4F5KQ

TEDx Talks: Epigenetics and the Influence of Our Genes: https://youtu.be/JTBg6hqeuTg

Environmental Determinants and Environmental Impacts on Health Resources

Agency for Toxic Substances and Disease Registry: Health Effects of Chemical Exposure: https://www.atsdr.cdc.gov/emes/public/docs/Health%20Effects%20of%20Chemical%20Exposure%20FS.pdf

Drexel News: Violent Crime Increases During Warmer Weather, No Matter the Season, Study Finds: https://drexel.edu/now/archive/2017/September/Violent-Crime-Increases-During-Warmer-Weather-No-Matter-the-Season/

EPA: Climate Change Indicators: Heat-Related Deaths: https://www.epa.gov/climate-indicators/climate-change-indicators-heat-related-deaths

EPA: Introduction to Indoor Air Quality: https://www.epa.gov/indoor-air-quality-iaq/introduction-indoor-air-quality

EPA. (June 22, 2022). *Textiles: material-specific data.* https://www.epa.gov/facts-and-figures-about-materials-waste-and-recycling/textiles-material-specific-data

JAMA Network: Impact of Changes in Transportation and Commuting Behaviors During the 1996 Summer Olympic Games in Atlanta on Air Quality and Childhood Asthma: https://jamanetwork.com/journals/jama/fullarticle/193572

NASA: The Effects of Climate Change: https://climate.nasa.gov/effects/

National Library of Medicine: A Time Series Analysis of Associations Between Daily Temperature and Crime Events in Philadelphia, Pennsylvania: https://pubmed.ncbi.nlm.nih.gov/28687898/

National Recreation and Park Association: Children in Nature: https://www.nrpa.org/uploadedFiles/nrpa.org/Advocacy/Children-in-Nature.pdf

NPR: Forest Bathing: A Retreat to Nature Can Boost Immunity And Mood: https://www.npr.org/sections/health-shots/2017/07/17/536676954/forest-bathing-a-retreat-to-nature-can-boost-immunity-and-mood

Pan American Health Organization: Environmental Determinants of Health: https://www.paho.org/en/topics/environmental-determinants-health

ScienceDirect: Environmental Impact of Textile Reuse and Recycling—A Review: https://www.sciencedirect.com/science/article/pii/S0959652618305985

Chronic Disease Prevention Resources

CDC: How You Can Prevent Chronic Diseases: https://www.cdc.gov/chronicdisease/about/prevent/index.htm

CDC: National Center for Chronic Disease Prevention and Health Promotion (NCCDPHP): https://www.cdc.gov/chronicdisease/index.htm

Cleveland Clinic: 5 Healthy Habits That Prevent Chronic Disease: https://health.clevelandclinic.org/5-healthy-habits-that-prevent-chronic-disease/

Harvard: 2 Ways to Protect Your Heart: Improve Sleep and Manage Stress: https://www.health.harvard.edu/healthbeat/2-ways-to-protect-your-heart-improve-sleep-and-manage-stress

National Library of Medicine: Inflammation: The Common Pathway of Stress-Related Diseases: https://www.ncbi.nlm.nih.gov/pmc/articles/PMC5476783/

National Prevention Council. (2011). *National Prevention Strategy: America's plan for better health and wellness.* U.S. Department of Health and Human Services. https://books.google.com/books?id=eTtkbEcg5P0C&lpg=PP1&pg=PP1#v=onepage&q&f=false

WHO: Dementia: https://www.who.int/news-room/fact-sheets/detail/dementia#:~:text=Rates%20of%20dementia,is%20between%205%2D8%25

Stress and Sleep Cycle Resources

American Psychological Association: Stress and Sleep: https://www.apa.org/news/press/releases/stress/2013/sleep

Harvard: Sleep and Mental Health: https://www.health.harvard.edu/newsletter_article/sleep-and-mental-health

Harvard: Sleep and Mood: https://healthysleep.med.harvard.edu/need-sleep/whats-in-it-for-you/mood#:~:text=Anxiety%20increases%20agitation%20and%20arousal,tend%20to%20have%20sleep%20problems

MedlinePlus: Sleep and Your Health: https://medlineplus.gov/ency/patientinstructions/000871.htm

National Library of Medicine: Extent and Health Consequences of Chronic Sleep Loss and Sleep Disorders: https://www.ncbi.nlm.nih.gov/books/NBK19961/

Sleep Foundation: Stress and Insomnia: https://www.sleepfoundation.org/insomnia/stress-and-insomnia

Sleep.org: Sleep and Stress: https://www.sleep.org/how-sleep-works/sleep-and-stress/

Social Isolation and Loneliness Resources

American Psychological Association: The Risks of Social Isolation: https://www.apa.org/monitor/2019/05/ce-corner-isolation

Berkeley: How Loneliness Hurts Us and What to Do About It: https://greatergood.berkeley.edu/article/item/how_loneliness_hurts_us_and_what_to_do_about_it

CDC: Loneliness and Social Isolation Linked to Serious Health Conditions: https://www.cdc.gov/aging/publications/features/lonely-older-adults.html

Harvard: Conquering Loneliness: https://www.health.harvard.edu/healthbeat/conquering-loneliness#:~:text=Loneliness%20and%20isolation%20can%20have,tasks%2C%20or%20an%20early%20death

National Institute on Aging: Loneliness and Social Isolation—Tips for Staying Connected: https://www.nia.nih.gov/health/loneliness-and-social-isolation-tips-staying-connected

Physical Activity Resources

American Psychological Association : The Exercise Effect: https://www.apa.org/monitor/2011/12/exercise

CDC: Benefits of Physical Activity: https://www.cdc.gov/physicalactivity/basics/pa-health/index.htm

CDC: Physical Activity Boosts Brain Health: https://www.cdc.gov/nccdphp/dnpao/features/physical-activity-brain-health/index.html

CDC: Physical Activity: Why It Matters: https://www.cdc.gov/physicalactivity/about-physical-activity/why-it-matters.html

Harvard: Better Balance: Activities to Keep You on an Even Keel : https://www.health.harvard.edu/staying-healthy/better-balance-activities-to-keep-you-on-an-even-keel

Harvard: Burning Calories Without Exercise: https://www.health.harvard.edu/staying-healthy/burning-calories-without-exercise

Harvard: How Simply Moving Benefits Your Mental Health: https://www.health.harvard.edu/blog/how-simply-moving-benefits-your-mental-health-201603289350

IHRSA: New Report: Exercise Plays Key Role in Mental Health & Well-being: https://www.ihrsa.org/improve-your-club/new-report-exercise-plays-key-role-in-mental-health-well-being/#

JAMA Network: Association of Step Volume and Intensity With All-Cause Mortality in Older Women: https://jamanetwork.com/journals/jamainternalmedicine/fullarticle/2734709?guestAccessKey=afffe229-3940-4dd1-94e6-56cdd109c457&utm_source=jps&utm_medium=email&utm_campaign=author_alert-jamanetwork&utm_content=author-author_engagement&utm_term=1m

Mayo Clinic: 10,000 Steps a Day: Too Low? Too High?: https://www.mayoclinic.org/healthy-lifestyle/fitness/in-depth/10000-steps/art-20317391

Mayo Clinic: Balance Exercises: https://www.mayoclinic.org/healthy-lifestyle/fitness/multimedia/balance-exercises/sls-20076853#:~:text=If%20you're%20an%20older,training%20in%20your%20regular%20activity

Mayo Clinic: Depression and Anxiety: Exercise Eases Symptoms: https://www.mayoclinic.org/diseases-conditions/depression/in-depth/depression-and-exercise/art-20046495

Mayo Clinic: The Importance of Movement: https://www.mayoclinichealthsystem.org/hometown-health/featured-topic/the-importance-of-movement

National Library of Medicine: Exercise for Mental Health: https://www.ncbi.nlm.nih.gov/pmc/articles/PMC1470658/

NIH: Number of Steps Per Day More Important Than Step Intensity: https://www.nih.gov/news-events/nih-research-matters/number-steps-day-more-important-step-intensity

U.S. Department of Health and Human Services: Physical Activity Guidelines for Americans: https://health.gov/sites/default/files/2019-09/Physical_Activity_Guidelines_2nd_edition.pdf

Screen Time Resources

American Academy of Child & Adolescent Psychiatry: Screen Time and Children: https://www.aacap.org/AACAP/Families_and_Youth/Facts_for_Families/FFF-Guide/Children-And-Watching-TV-054.aspx

Berkeley: How to Protect Kids From Nature-Deficit Disorder: https://greatergood.berkeley.edu/article/item/how_to_protect_kids_from_nature_deficit_disorder

BMJ Open: *Effects of Screentime on the Health and Well-being of Children and Adolescents: A Systematic Review of Reviews*: https://bmjopen.bmj.com/content/9/1/e023191

Harvard: Screen Time and the Brain: https://hms.harvard.edu/news/screen-time-brain

Louv, R. (2008). *Last child in the woods: Saving our children from nature-deficit disorder*. Algonquin Books. https://books.google.com/books?hl=en&lr=&id=WnLBBwAAQBAJ&oi=fnd&pg=PP1&dq=nature+deficit+disorder&ots=XCAwvM3Oyf&sig=LrTToimhThFkGC-6iLTPOe5QqQs#v=onepage&q=nature%20deficit%20disorder&f=false

Mayo Clinic: 5 Ways Slimming Screentime Is Good for Your Health: https://mcpress.mayoclinic.org/healthletter/5-ways-slimming-screentime-is-good-for-your-health/

Mayo Clinic: Children and Screen Time: How Much Is Too Much?: https://www.mayoclinichealthsystem.org/hometown-health/speaking-of-health/children-and-screen-time

MedlinePlus: Screen Time and Children: https://medlineplus.gov/ency/patientinstructions/000355.htm

National Library of Medicine: Associations Between Screen Time and Lower Psychological Well-being Among Children and Adolescents: Evidence From a Population-based Study: https://www.ncbi.nlm.nih.gov/pmc/articles/PMC6214874/

Nutrition Resources

American Diabetes Association: Diet Soda Intake and Risk of Incident Metabolic Syndrome and Type 2 Diabetes in the Multi-Ethnic Study of Atherosclerosis (MESA): https://diabetesjournals.org/care/article/32/4/688/29040/Diet-Soda-Intake-and-Risk-of-Incident-Metabolic

American Heart Association: Added Sugars: https://www.heart.org/en/healthy-living/healthy-eating/eat-smart/sugar/added-sugars

American Heart Association *Circulation*: Dietary Sugars Intake and Cardiovascular Health: https://www.ahajournals.org/doi/10.1161/circulationaha.109.192627

American Heart Association: How Much Sodium Should I Eat Per Day?: https://www.heart.org/en/healthy-living/healthy-eating/eat-smart/sodium/how-much-sodium-should-i-eat-per-day

Harvard: Added Sugar: https://www.hsph.harvard.edu/nutrition
source/carbohydrates/added-sugar-in-the-diet/#:~:text=The%20
AHA%20suggests%20an%20added,of%20sugar

National Library of Medicine: Food Insecurity Is Associated With Obesity Among US Adults in 12 States: https://www.ncbi.nlm.nih.gov/pmc/articles/PMC4584410/

National Library of Medicine: The Food-Insecurity Obesity Paradox: A Resource-Scarcity Hypothesis: https://www.ncbi.nlm.nih.gov/pmc/articles/PMC5394740/

National Library of Medicine: Food Swamps Predict Obesity Rates Better Than Food Deserts in the United States: https://www.ncbi.nlm.nih.gov/pmc/articles/PMC5708005/

NIH: Portion Distortion: https://www.nhlbi.nih.gov/health/educational/wecan/eat-right/portion-distortion.htm

ScienceDirect: Daily Bingeing on Sugar Repeatedly Releases Dopamine in the Accumbens Shell: https://www.sciencedirect.com/science/article/abs/pii/S0306452205004288?via%3Dihub

University of California San Francisco: Sugar Science: https://sugarscience.ucsf.edu/

USDA: Characteristics and Influential Factors of Food Deserts: https://www.ers.usda.gov/webdocs/publications/45014/30940_err140.pdf

USDA: Dietary Guidelines for Americans: https://www.dietaryguidelines.gov/sites/default/files/2020-12/Dietary_Guidelines_for_Americans_2020-2025.pdf

USDA: MyPlate: https://www.myplate.gov/

Behavior Change Theory Resources

Boston University: The Transtheoretical Model (Stages of Change): https://sphweb.bumc.bu.edu/otlt/mph-modules/sb/behavioralchangetheories/behavioralchangetheories6.html

Hayden, J. (2019). *Introduction to health behavior theory* (3rd ed.). Jones & Bartlett Learning.

APPENDIX

VALUES LIST

Choose your top 15 values from the list below. Then, whittle that list down to your top 10. Finally, choose your top 5 from those remaining. Go back to page 131 and write down your top 5 values and a note to yourself about why you chose those specific values.

1. Acceptance: to be accepted as I am
2. Accuracy: to be accurate in my opinions and beliefs
3. Achievement: to have important accomplishments
4. Adventure: to have new and exciting experiences
5. Attractiveness: to be physically attractive
6. Authority: to be in charge of and responsible for others
7. Autonomy: to be self-determined and independent
8. Beauty: to appreciate beauty around me
9. Caring: to take care of others
10. Challenge: to take on difficult tasks and problems
11. Change: to have a life full of change and variety
12. Comfort: to have a pleasant and comfortable life
13. Commitment: to make enduring, meaningful commitments

14. Compassion: to feel and act on concern for others
15. Contribution: to make a lasting contribution in the world
16. Cooperation: to work collaboratively with others
17. Courtesy: to be considerate and polite toward others
18. Creativity: to have new and original ideas
19. Dependability: to be reliable and trustworthy
20. Duty: to carry out my duties and obligations
21. Ecology: to live in harmony with the environment
22. Excitement: to have a life full of thrills and stimulation
23. Faithfulness: to be loyal and true in relationships
24. Fame: to be known and recognized
25. Family: to have a happy, loving family
26. Fitness: to be physically fit and strong
27. Flexibility: to adjust to new circumstances easily
28. Forgiveness: to be forgiving of others
29. Friendship: to have close, supportive friends
30. Fun: to play and have fun
31. Generosity: to give what I have to others
32. Genuineness: to act in a manner that is true to who I am
33. God's will: to seek and obey the will of God
34. Growth: to keep changing and growing
35. Health: to be physically well and healthy
36. Helpfulness: to be helpful to others
37. Honesty: to be honest and truthful
38. Hope: to maintain a positive and optimistic outlook
39. Humility: to be modest and unassuming
40. Humor: to see the humorous side of myself and the world
41. Independence: to be free from dependence on others
42. Industry: to work hard and well at my life tasks
43. Inner peace: to experience personal peace

44. Intimacy: to share my innermost experiences with others
45. Justice: to promote fair and equal treatment for all
46. Knowledge: to learn and contribute valuable knowledge
47. Leisure: to take time to relax and enjoy
48. Loved: to be loved by those close to me
49. Loving: to give love to others
50. Mastery: to be competent in my everyday activities
51. Mindfulness: to live conscious and mindful of the present moment
52. Moderation: to avoid excesses and find a middle ground
53. Monogamy: to have one close, loving relationship
54. Non-conformity: to question and challenge authority and norms
55. Nurturance: to take care of and nurture others
56. Openness: to be open to new experiences, ideas, and opinions
57. Order: to have a life that is well-ordered and organized
58. Passion: to have deep feelings about ideas, activities, or people
59. Pleasure: to feel good
60. Popularity: to be well-liked by many people
61. Power: to have control over others
62. Purpose: to have meaning and direction in my life
63. Rationality: to be guided by reason and logic
64. Realism: to see and act realistically and practically
65. Responsibility: to make and carry out responsible decisions
66. Risk: to take risks and chances
67. Romance: to have intense, exciting love in my life
68. Safety: to be safe and secure
69. Self-Acceptance: to accept myself as I am

70. Self-control: to be disciplined in my own actions
71. Self-esteem: to feel good about myself
72. Self-knowledge: to have a deep and honest understanding of myself
73. Service: to be of service to others
74. Sexuality: to have an active and satisfying sex life
75. Simplicity: to live life simply, with minimal needs
76. Solitude: to have time and space where I can be apart from others
77. Spirituality: to grow and mature spiritually
78. Stability: to have a life that stays fairly consistent
79. Tolerance: to accept and respect those who differ from me
80. Tradition: to follow respected patterns of the past
81. Virtue: to live a morally pure and excellent life
82. Wealth: to have plenty of money
83. World Peace: to work to promote peace in the world